Twayne's United States Authors Series

SYLVIA E. BOWMAN, *Editor*

INDIANA UNIVERSITY

Phyllis McGinley

PHYLLIS McGINLEY

By LINDA WELSHIMER WAGNER

Michigan State University

TUSAS 170

Twayne Publishers, Inc. :: New York

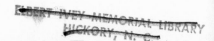

The writings of Phyllis McGinley reproduced in this book are quoted with the permission of their respective publishers and are copyrighted as follows:

A Pocketful of Wry (New York: Duell, Sloan and Pearce, Inc.) copyright © 1940, 1959 by Phyllis McGinley;

The Province of the Heart (New York: The Viking Press, Inc.) copyright © 1959 by Phyllis McGinley.

Sixpence in Her Shoe (New York: The Macmillan Co.) copyright © 1960, 1962, 1963, 1964 by Phyllis McGinley.

Stones from a Glass House (New York: The Viking Press, Inc.) copyright © 1941, copyright © renewed 1969 by Phyllis McGinley; some poems originally appearing in *The New Yorker;*

Times Three (New York: The Viking Press, Inc.) copyright © each year 1932-1960 by Phyllis McGinley; some poems originally appearing in *The New Yorker;*

The writings of Denise Levertov and William Carlos Williams reproduced in this book are quoted with the permission of New Directions Publishing Corporation and are copyrighted as follows:

O Taste and See. Copyright © 1964 by Denise Levertov Goodman.

Pictures from Brueghel and Other Poems. Copyright © 1962 by William Carlos Williams. Both reprinted by permission of New Directions Publishing Corporation.

For Doug and Tom, "walking strange waters"

"One must always tell what one sees. Above all, which is more difficult, one must always see what one sees."

Charles Péguy

Preface

In writing about a modern author like Phyllis McGinley, the critic has a double responsibility: to discuss the writing itself and its relationship with other contemporary work. Such is the primary purpose of this book about Miss McGinley, who is, however, more than a modern poet. She is—in many ways—a public institution, a public voice. Millions of readers know her views; millions more recognize her name. In this age of largely private poetry and clique poets, in this age of faddish and sporadic reading, Phyllis McGinley has a following—a large following— of actual readers. In this age when "no publisher makes money on poetry," McGinley's books sell a hundred thousand copies.

Because Miss McGinley's work is so widely read, I think any student of it should be unusually conscious of the time, the society, the milieu from which it arose—and which it influenced. Sometimes her prose and poetry have a direct tie with a newspaper headline; or they relate to an issue in the public eye— teenage dating, progressive education, the many phases of war or poverty. Often too, of course, McGinley's writing relates only to the world of McGinley—as mother, wife, neighbor, or simply as woman.

Miss McGinley herself is something rather rare in twentieth- century literature, or so the social observers would have us believe. She is a woman who speaks her mind—and not a bad mind at that. She believes firmly in religion, in personal morality, in the beauty of fine, old things and of the finest of old principles. She responds to sympathy, enjoys nature, worries about her children, grows impatient with trivia—and trivial people. McGin- ley enjoys good living, but not at the expense of other values or of other personalities. No paragon, no exemplar, no saint, she is a person—full, idiosyncratic, just, understanding, witty, recog- nizable.

Readers identify with her (the one fault of art today is that it has grown away from the people); readers laugh with her; they condone and admire her. They say, "Oh, Phyllis McGinley— yes, yes, I *know* her." And in a very real sense they do, for she comes through vividly in much of her writing. So we have an identity, a Phyllis McGinley. And, we have an identity that is approachable. Being enthusiastic, believing that her husband loves her, struggling to get the errands done before lunchtime—most readers, not only women readers, understand and approve these attitudes. The goals of the contemporary poet who wants isolation for his life or narcotics for his pleasure are much less meaningful to most of us. Social attitudes are no criteria on which to judge a person's poetry, but they eventually determine how wide an audience one reaches. (Poems usually reflect themes important to the poet; his social attitudes cannot help but influence what things he finds important.) The most essential quality of Phyllis McGinley, poet, is not, however, her approachability—not her humor. It is, simply, her poetic skill.

Miss McGinley has published widely and has been honored frequently because she is a good poet. She writes with a technical proficiency equal to that of the best-known poets through history. She knows how to use the full range of poetic devices; and she writes with the freedom, the innovation, possible only after a person has thoroughly mastered the ground rules of an art. Her forty years of poetry show that McGinley learned early the craft of the poem. I suppose it is this reciprocity of abilities that makes Phyllis McGinley the outstanding literary figure she is: her humanity infuses her technically adept poem; and her respect for workmanship keeps even her most emotional poems from being mawkish.

In this book, I shall try to illuminate the above statements through intensive reading of McGinley's poetry and prose. Chapter 1 presents several poems which seem to represent the major categories within McGinley's poetry. Taken from her work during the 1950's, poems such as "Song of High Cuisine," "Lament for Lost Lodgings," and "The Doll House" illustrate McGinley's range of technical effects and of thematic concerns.

Chapter 2 attempts to define the elusive term "light verse," with forays into the history of that genre, its prominence early in this century, and its present standing. I have included many selections from the work of other light-verse writers in the hope of giving the reader some small basis for comparison. One section of this chapter also looks briefly at modern "serious" poetry.

Chapters 3, 4, 5, and 6 consider McGinley's writing chronologically, by decade, as she divided her 1960 selected poems, *Times Three*. Chapter 3 refers to poetry written during the late 1920's and the 1930's; Chapter 4 considers the poetry of the

Preface

1940's, as well as the three children's books published in those
years. Chapter 5 surveys poetry, children's books, and essays
from the 1950's. Chapter 6 discusses all work since 1960, including
the Pulitzer Prize-winning *Times Three* and the 1967 *A Wreath
of Christmas Legends*. Chapter 6 includes a summation of the
trends evidenced through these nearly forty years of writing,
as well as this author's critical position.

Each chapter includes as much primary material as possible—
poems and excerpts from prose, explicated where possible with
McGinley's own relevant comments. My thanks go to Miss
McGinley for her cooperation, and for her permission to use
the materials here included. Thanks go also to her publishers
Crowell-Collier; Doubleday, Doran, and Company; Duell, Sloan,
and Pearce; Harcourt, Brace Company; J. B. Lippincott; The
Macmillan Company; Viking Press; and Franklin Watts.

Materials from the Lockwood Memorial Library Poetry Collection, State University of New York at Buffalo, and the Syracuse
University Library Collection are used by permission of those
libraries.

Michigan State University   LINDA WELSHIMER WAGNER
East Lansing, Michigan

Contents

Chronology

1905   Phyllis Louise McGinley born in Ontario, Oregon, on March 21, daughter of Daniel McGinley and Julia Kiesel McGinley. Moved at three months to a Colorado ranch.

1917   Father died. Moved to Ogden, Utah, where Phyllis attended Sacred Heart Academy and Odgen High School.

1927   Graduated from University of Utah; taught school.

1929   Taught English in New Rochelle, New York; began publishing poetry.

1935   *On the Contrary.*

1936   Married Charles L. Hayden.

1937   *One More Manhattan.*

1939   Daughter Julie born.

1940   *A Pocketful of Wry.*

1941   Daughter Patsy born; *Husbands Are Difficult.*

1944   *The Horse Who Lived Upstairs.*

1945   *The Plain Princess.*

1946   *Stones from a Glass House.*

1948   *All Around the Town* and *A Name for Kitty;* wrote lyrics for the Broadway revue, *Small Wonder.*

1950   *The Most Wonderful Doll in the World.*

1951   *Blunderbus, The Horse Who Had His Picture in the Paper,* and *A Short Walk from the Station.* Wrote continuity for the movie *The Emperor's Nightingale.*

1953   *The Make-Believe Twins.*

1954   *The Love Letters of Phyllis McGinley,* which won the Edna St. Vincent Millay Memorial Award.

1955   Elected to the National Institute of Arts and Letters.

1957   *The Year Without a Santa Claus.*

1958   *Merry Christmas, Happy New Year.*

1959   *The Province of the Heart, Lucy McLockett.*

1960   *Times Three* (selected poems), *Sugar and Spice.*

1961   Awarded Pulitzer Prize for *Times Three; Mince Pie and Mistletoe.*

1962   *Boys Are Awful; The B Book.*

1963 *A Girl and Her Room; How Mrs. Santa Claus Saved Christmas.*
1964 *Sixpence in Her Shoe.*
1965 Read at White House Arts Festival.
1966 *Wonderful Time.*
1967 *A Wreath of Christmas Legends.*
1968 *Wonders and Surprises.*
1969 *Saint-Watching*

CHAPTER 1

Of Types and Triolets

I *"Typical"* McGinley

POETS, like any other public performers, can easily become typed. One kind of poem, one insistent theme, one predominant image—and readers think automatically of the writer as so marked. In modern poetry, the satiric couplet belongs to Ogden Nash; the lengthy catalogue reminds one of Whitman; the flower asphodel suggests William Carlos Williams. And—for several reasons—poems like "Song of High Cuisine" are often associated with Phyllis McGinley:

> At Bloomingdale's,
> At Bloomingdale's,
>   Who would not wish to be—
> Where hornéd are the Gallic Snails,
>   Where curls the anchovy!
> For palate stales as winter fails
>   And rainy spring comes on.
> So they have birds at Bloomingdale's
>   That flew in Carcassonne.

> Yes, hark!
> The lark
> At heaven's gate,
>   That lately sang so pure,
> There trussed and truffled for the plate
>   Invites the epicure. . . .[1]

"Song of High Cuisine" is, first of all, a clever poem. McGinley has been writing the most polished of light verse ever since the late 1920's, when she discovered that *The New Yorker* paid higher rates for "light" poetry than for "serious." That there was a demand for light verse was the important consideration to this young English teacher-turned-writer. She wanted to live from her writing; obviously, she needed a market.

15

The 1920's were the great age of light, satiric verse (see Chapter 2). Samuel Hoffenstein, Dorothy Parker, FPA, Christopher Morley, Arthur Guiterman, Ogden Nash, and A. P. Herbert—they were the popular poets. Ezra Pound and T. S. Eliot were being published in foreign countries; W. C. Williams, Hart Crane and Wallace Stevens were being published by small, private presses. Then, as now, there were many more poets than markets for poetry. For the writers of light verse, however, newspapers provided an almost inexhaustible demand. The popular city papers used columns of light verse, many on a daily basis. The papers could consequently buy and buy and buy— and, perhaps more important, people could read and read and read.

The present market of the 1960's for light verse is much more limited. At least partly because of space shortages, much modern light verse takes the form of quatrains or couplets. Technically, it is a long way from the couplet to longer, intricate poems like "Song of High Cuisine." The alternate rhyme pattern—demanding in its own right—is expanded here in the second and third stanzas to include additional lines. It is difficult, however, to see where the lines have been added to the original nine-line verse. Each of the three stanzas opens with a pair of short rhyming lines. These couplets are followed by the body of the stanza, lines which rhyme *abab*, and in some cases interlock further. Rhythm is iambic tetrameter and trimeter, with variation in rhythm correlating with the variation in rhyme. The opening of the second stanza, for example, "Yes, hark!/ The lark/ At heaven's gate," breaks the rhyme scheme in that *hark* and *lark* do not rhyme with any words used later in the stanza. These short lines also break the rhythmic pattern by containing only one accented syllable. Emphasis results from the slow, end-rhyming lines, an emphasis which helps to give the poem an effective pause after the regular movement of the first stanza.

The second passage of variation concludes the poem:

> Ah, few the sales
> At Bloomingdale's,
>   Amid imported straw,
> Of tongues of foreign nightingales
>   Or pearls in Malaga.
> But they have many a merry thing.
>   So who'll go there to buy
> The little larks with parsleyed wing

That speak so eloquent of spring,
The single thrush that does not sing?

Well, gentlemen, not I.

The middle lines of this excerpt are iambic tetrameter, instead of alternating long and short lines. This recurrent beat helps the poem build to a climax, especially when the question is followed by space before the last, shorter line. The change of pace achieved here helps to prepare the reader for the negative ending.

Conducive to greater skepticism, too, is the insistent rhyme of *wing, spring, sing*. Even though the repetition in sound adds to the speed of these three tetrameter lines, the words in themselves create more irony for the poem's subject—the dead, marketable birds. *Wing, spring, sing*, all usually associated with living birds, are of no consequence to grocery-list items.

With her adroit handling of poetic devices throughout the poem, McGinley has already "said" what she finally states as conclusion. The opening stanza does more than give the situation; for, by mentioning the season of "rainy spring" and the fact that "winter fails," McGinley prepares the reader's mind for thoughts of birds—live birds. Her first stanza does not, in fact, make clear the condition of the birds in question: "So they have birds at Bloomingdale's/ That flew in Carcassonne." In stanza two, plosives are used in describing the dead larks—"trussed and truffled for the plate/ Invites the epicure." The sound of these lines contrasts suitably with the following softer section in which McGinley relies on assonance and sibilance:

And, sheltering from the Alpine wind
In more than Alpine hush,
Arrives most elegantly tinned
A solitary thrush.

The ironic opening of the second stanza and the understatement of "more than Alpine hush" are obvious signals for the ending, as are the contradictory lines from stanza three, "few the sales/ At Bloomingdale's" and "But they have many a merry thing." The word *merry* strikes a discordant note. The situation is in no way merry unless in the sense of carnival or burlesque. These birds "that speak so eloquently of spring" are far from merry, dead. And as the poet says, with firmness (and with rhyme), "So who'll go there to buy . . . / Well, gentlemen, not I."

"Song of High Cuisine" is good light verse—one clue that

McGinley is its author. The poem also is a New York poem, and
McGinley is usually thought of as a New Yorker. Her early life
was spent in the West—Oregon, Colorado, Utah—but at twenty-
four she went to New York to teach high-school English; and in
a few years she became a free-lance writer. She then became an
editorial writer; later she wrote copy for an advertising agency
and helped to edit *Town and Country*. Since her marriage in 1936,
she has lived in suburban areas of the city in both New York
state and Connecticut.

Another reason for identifying Miss McGinley with this poem
is her sex. A woman would be somewhat more interested than
a man in the subject of "Song"—in both its culinary and esthetic
aspects. "Song" is also a timely poem, and McGinley is known
for her use of contemporary materials. As the prefatory note
to the poem tells, McGinley had read in the *New York Times*
that the birds were for sale; indeed, she often uses quotations
from the news as epigraphs for poems. Ostensibly, then, many of
McGinley's poems are "current"; they have the flavor of 1954,
1931, or 1969. As this particular poem shows, however, the year
in which it was written is relatively unimportant. The much-
prized flavor of contemporaneity stems more from McGinley's
underlying theme than it does from any dated copy of the
Times—themes like: (1) What does it take to appease, to attract,
men? (2) In a world where foreign delicacies are only hours
away, where can men go for their "merry" satisfactions? And, by
implication, (3) are these dead birds the chief prizes of Car-
cassone and the French Alps?

But it is much pleasanter to find the themes in McGinley's
poetry than in my prose. Admittedly, one strength of poetry is
that it *shows* instead of telling, that by involving the mind of a
reader, it can lead him through to conclusions of his own—
subtly, even indirectly—without being didactic. This approach
is McGinley's forte. As she says of her poetry, "There's a hell
of a lot of straight social criticism."[2] Readers, however, tend to
think first of humor and polish when they think of Phyllis
McGinley: she is no H. L. Mencken; she certainly raises no
Allen Ginsberg "howl." But her censure of society, her willingness
to take unpopular stands when they are necessary, is clear—
whether the issues are slight or weighty.

"Lament for Lost Lodgings" is a good example of McGinley's
apt social criticism. The poem begins with an epigraph from
Hilaire Belloc's "Tarantella": "Do you remember an Inn,

Miranda?" The poem proper continues the conversation with the lady. The tone of address and the name *Miranda* both fit the mood McGinley is trying to create—of old-time, unhurried luxury and pleasure:

> Yes, do you remember an Inn,
> Miranda,
> Where chairs rocked, creaking,
> On the long veranda,
> Where beds were elderly
> To match the plumbing
> But the manager smiled at our coming?
>
> (56)

The balancing pauses—*Miranda* set by itself in line two and the commas separating *creaking* from the rest of the context—slow the tempo even more.

As in so many of McGinley's poems, she uses, as in "Lament," the catalogue of items. Her catalogues are always more than lists, however, thanks to the well-chosen adjective, the isolated bit of pertinent information:

> Remember the lobster redder than the wine,
> The breakfast dining-room
> That closed at nine,
> The wavy mirrors
> In the first-floor Women's,
> The waitresses all from Smith or Simmons
> And the crickets loud
> But the busboys louder. . . .

The dining room that closes at nine, for example, is indicative of several things: one, a culture in which people do not loaf in bed all morning; two, a technology—or lack of it—which requires that the chef spend several hours preparing for lunch, perhaps in the European tradition.

Then, in contrasting tone, McGinley begins her description of the modern tourist's accommodations—with the familiar line from "The Raven."

> Nevermore, Miranda, nevermore.
> Only the faceless,
> Duplicated door
> Of a thousand Motels
> From Taos to Truro
> With Television built in the built-in bureau.

> Only the wallpaper, self-assertive,
> And the dusty coming
> And the going, furtive. . . .

Up to this point, McGinley's capitalization has been standard, so
that the impact of *Television*, capitalized as it is after *Taos* and
Truro, is strong. The God of modern society deserves upper case,
or so the poet's form ironically suggests. The repetition of *built-in*
is also amusingly accurate. Everything *is* built in; there is little
difference between one room and the next. "Only the faceless/
Duplicated door" represents—not McGinley's beloved privacy,
as references to doors so often do—but disinterest. She has realized
in her travels that the once-cherished gift of hospitality has become one of the world's biggest sales gimmicks, with "the fee in
advance, please." And so she pleads,

> Let me fly to an Inn like a sword to its scabbard
> Where the crickets cry
> And the walls are clapboard.
> Till I find a rocker
> On a long veranda
> I'll motor no more, Miranda.

Again, this poem is clever, timely, and critical; but the basis
for criticism is a positive one: McGinley has known a better
way, and she writes from that vantage point. Again she uses the
alternating quatrain and couplet pattern (*abcbdd*), although
the pattern is far from rigid. She uses inversion to intensify
rhythm or create a rhyme: "And the dusty coming/ And the going,
furtive." The rhythm is a combination of two-and-three-stress
feet, chiefly anapestic. This rhythm is more indicative of motion
than is straight iambic. It permits the poem to cover more ground,
so to speak.

So, McGinley is critical of canned birds and noisy motels. To
most readers, these are not monumental topics, yet they are
symptomatic. Most people do not live with war mongers or
saints; they see the goodness or the decadence in life through
its details, through the trivia of daily existence. And of these
kinds of telling details McGinley often writes. I do not mean to
imply, however, that Miss McGinley has not been concerned
with warmongering or sainthood. As her poems on wide ranges of
subjects show, she writes on themes that are meaningful to her.

In this respect, one of McGinley's most interesting series of
poems is the group entitled "Reformers, Saints, and Preachers."

As a Catholic herself, she knows enough about the personalities she treats to be accurate and fair. However, she is not always as serious as some authorities might wish her to be. She sees the human side, and often the human side is a funny side—in even these revered figures. Of "Simeon Stylites," who sat on the desert pillar for thirty years, she writes:

> And why did Simeon sit like that,
> Without a garment,
> Without a hat,
> In a holy rage
> For the world to see?
> It puzzles the age,
> It puzzled many
> A Desert Father.
> And I think it puzzled the Good Lord, rather.
>
> (30)

And of the bountiful Saint Bridget, McGinley declares:

> Well, one must love her.
> Nonetheless,
> In thinking of her
> Givingness,
> There's no denial
> She must have been
> A sort of trial
> To her kin.
> The moral, too, seems rather quaint.
> *Who* had the patience of a saint,
> From evidence presented here?
> Saint Bridget? Or her near and dear?
>
> (22)

The repetitions, slant rhymes, and short rhythms help to reflect the tone the poet intends. McGinley defines her levity in the second part of "Two Sides of Calvin," subtitled "A Rondeau for Geneva, 1542." This poem expresses the poet's view of a harshly staid society, where "mirth won little or no renown":

> Nobody laughed much. None might sing
> Or dance to fiddles or kiss-and-cling.
> Condemned together were lover and clown
> In the City of God.
>
> For smiling in church, or slumbering,
> For wreathing a Maypole come the Spring,

Jail was the punishment handed down.
One wonders if God, when He walked the town,
Ever felt homesick or anything
In the City of God.

(28)

This poem, like the very fine "Sonnet from Assisi" and the
intricately rhyming "Lesson for Beginners," which also appear
in this sequence, shows McGinley's control of the most rigid
verse forms. The rondeau, as it originated in France, early in
the sixteenth century, consists of thirteen lines divided into three
stanzas of five, three, and five lines. At the close of the second
and third stanzas appear the *rentrement* (partial repetition),
a refrain composed of the first few words of the poem—in this
case, "In the City of God." Only two end rhymes are used
throughout the entire poem. Here, McGinley uses *king, fling,*
and the various *-ing* words, and *down, town, renown,* etc. The
rhyme pattern is *aabba, aabR, aabbaR.* Each line is to contain
eight or ten syllables; McGinley's have eight, nine, or ten, with
the opening line of a section usually being longer (here, ten
syllables).

The significant point about McGinley's near-perfect rondeau
is, I think, that she has managed to keep a contemporary flavor
within the limiting confines of form. "Nobody laughed much"
is modern in its abruptness, as are the poignant closing lines.
The phrase "or anything"—besides being justified through rhyme
requirements—is a masterful play on the lameness of twentieth-
century speech . . . these are not the days of the positive Calvin.
This description is not the sure, precise one that a dogmatist
would have used—and for one important reason: McGinley does
not pretend to know what God felt; she just suggests, "One
wonders." Her lameness is partially a representation of man's
awe before his Creator. The repetition of *God* in the *rentrement*
reinforces the irony: perhaps God, too, is lost and lonely since
Calvin has become "king" of His city.

McGinley's twenty poems on saints, reformers, and preachers
are very different in technique and tone; but they share one
important trait—each poem emphasizes the humanity in the
character portrayed. These are men and women, not coldly
isolated wraiths from history. And the poems are vivid because
each has an unmistakable focus, an apt detail which, owing to
the poet's limiting of the characterization, gives it strength. Both
McGinley's perception of character and her dramatic ability to

choose a telling detail are evident in this gallery of poems (see pp. 106-9 for other work in this theme.)

II *And Others*

These, then, are some of the "typically McGinley" poems—polished satire, humorous censure, perceptive characterization. There are many other poems that differ from these in being more personal because they are written on themes which seem to be closer to the poet. These are the poems of children, of husband, of home, and of McGinley herself. Recently, McGinley's writing has indicated that she has a strong pride in and a deep reliance on her sex. The woman's role in life provides many of the subjects—and the larger, underlying themes—for McGinley's later work, as her 1959 collection of essays shows. *The Province of the Heart* has to do with "the honor of being a woman" in various roles—mother, wife, companion, hostess, gardner, career woman. The 1963 *Sixpence in Her Shoe* relates more particularly to the pleasures, duties, and skills of housewifery. Although McGinley's comments about men in these essays are both fond and apt, her focus is woman—and the qualities which make her the creature she is. As she writes in "Some of My Best Friends . . .": "I like women . . ."

I like them for their all-around, all-weather dependability. I like them because they are generally so steady, realistic, and careful about tidying up after a hot shower. I admire them for their prudence, thrift, gallantry, common sense, and knobless knees, and because they are neither so vain nor so given to emotion as their opposite numbers. I like the way they answer letters promptly, put shoe trees in their shoes at night, and are so durable physically. Their natures may not be so fine or their hearts so readily touched as man's, but they are not so easily imposed on either.[3]

Gifted with common sense and self-reliance, woman, as McGinley identifies her, is also a realist; she is perceptive to the worlds around her and to the relationships within them. Some of McGinley's best poems have to do with these personal relationships. In "Girl's-Eye View of Relatives," for example, she describes fathers as "dragon-seekers, bent on improbable rescues," always "the worriers." "Girl's-Eye View" is a sequence of five poems, the last two of which are especially interesting. The fourth poem is the girl's view of her aunts; the fifth, of her mother. The contrast between the two poems is masterfully handled. "In Praise of

Aunts" is forty lines long; "The Adversary," (about the mother,)
four. The long, casual praise builds easily from five- and six-line
stanzas to eight-, nine-, and ten-line verses before the single-
line imperative which closes the poem: "All should have aunts,
or else adopt one." The virtues of the beloved aunts are those
of moderation, and this quality is phrased in the cool understatement of the young viewer: "Aunts are discreet, a little shy/
By instinct." "Aunts care, but only mildly care,/ About our
winter moods." "Aunts carry no duty in their faces."

The quatrain about the mother is abrupt in its understatement,
but all the more poignant for its brevity. The title, "The Adversary," is followed immediately by the declaration, "A mother's
hardest to forgive." The rest of the poem explains why the
mother is an adversary, *the* adversary, in fact:

> A mother's hardest to forgive.
> Life is the fruit she longs to hand you,
> Ripe on a plate. And while you live,
> Relentlessly she understands you.
>
> (44)

That aunts, like their poem, are casual ("lenient but cool") is
indicated in McGinley's use of the iambic couplets through most
of the poem. The regular rhythm adds to the humorously fond
tone. Some of the rhymes are slant, and some are extended for
three lines to give the poem some necessary variation.

"The Doll House," one of McGinley's best-known poems, shows
further insight into the mother-child relationship or, perhaps,
into any relationship of mutability. The doll house stands as a
symbol of permanence in a world of shifting values and loves.
McGinley seems to deify it because it is "incorruptible":

> There was nothing much
> That couldn't be used again with a bit of repair.
> It was all there,
> Perfect and little and inviolate.

Once it had been loaned to the children; now hers, the house
gives her "grave delight." And, since the children have gone, she
realizes

> Always, from the beginning,
> This outcome had been clear. Ah! She had known
> Since the first clapboard was fitted, first rafter hung
> (Yet not till now had known that she had known),

This was no daughters' fortune but her own—
Something cautiously lent to the careless young.
. . . .
Now all would thrive.

Over this house, most tranquil and complete,
Where no storm ever beat,
Whose innocent stair
No messenger ever climbed on quickened feet
With tidings either of rapture or of despair,
She was sole mistress. Through the panes she was able
To peer at her world reduced to the size of dream
But pure and unaltering.

(53-55)

The poem continues: the fire will not turn cold, the heart will
never tire, the spring will never pass—nothing will ever grow old.
    "The Doll House" is one of very few McGinley poems written
in a freer meter, a near blank verse. The closeness of the subject
seems to have demanded a more natural rhythm—one more
conversational, as if the poet were speaking the poem:

It was a good house. It had been artfully built
By an idle carpenter once, when the times were duller.
The windows opened and closed. The knocker was gilt . . .

She brought it down once more
To a bedroom, empty now, on the second floor
And put the furniture in.

Both quotations express the fact that changes have come (the
bedroom is empty now, times are busier) just as the long excerpt
on page 24 indicates that the children are now young ladies.
"The Doll House" is thematically as much about the passing of
time—and, by implication, about the changes in a mother's life—
as it is about a child's toy. Yet McGinley expertly avoids the traps
inherent in such topics—triteness, excessive sentiment—through
her ostensible focus on the doll house. Description is accurate
and minute: the narrator's painstaking care is itself a revelation
of her love for the toy: "She squandered/ One bold October day
and half the night/ Binding the carpets round with a ribbon
border."
    Another theme suggested in this poem is the conflict among a
household of women: "Wholly her gift at last,/ Here was her
private estate"; "She was sole mistress." That there had been

differences of opinion is implied in her comment that there was no one "to trespass, no one to mock/ The extravagance of her sewing or her spending." There were no "careless young."

But why does the "seed of the past" flower so "fearfully"? She has the house, her world reduced to a miniature dream. She has a respite in "this web of quietness/ Where there was neither After nor Before." The fearfulness comes, I think, from the same origin as her *wry* thought that she had always coveted the doll house, that she had designed it, cared for it, and given it only "cautiously" to her children. The house was her attempt to capture order, to capture and hold life. But, once she had captured it, what then? And even as she "reached her hand to stroke the unwithering grasses/ Besides the small and incorruptible door," the reader feels that she also knows that this house is a dream. The fearful flowering of time has brought the changes the mother both anticipated and dreaded: her children are gone.

Miss McGinley, writing in the 1965 *American Scholar*, calls "The Doll House" her "intimation of morality," unquestionably "serious in content" but light "in its piling up of domestic details." Of its form, she writes, "The poem's shape, as it should always do, hinged on its content. I planned it as narration, almost a short story. Therefore the tone had to be conversational rather than animated. Therefore, again, meter should be loose and rhyme unobstrusive. If I had been braver I might well have left out rhyme entirely. But I have traded so long in my speciality that I feel safer with rhyming guidelines. I did, though, try to disguise them. . . ."[4] And this emphasis on the poem as an organic form shows us again McGinley as true poet, expressing in her attention to shape the love of the craftsman for his perfectly honed product (a love not unlike that of the homemaker for the perfectly restored doll house).

CHAPTER 2

Light Verse: The Anomaly

I *Definition and Perspectives*

BETTE Richart, writing in *The Commonweal*, considers "The Doll House" to be one of McGinley's best poems; in fact, an excellent one. However her general opinion is that Miss McGinley is too often "merely flippant," that she glorifies the "common" instead of the significant values of the commonplace.[1] Perhaps this kind of criticism is inherent when we consider light verse. Light verse—impossibly broad term that it is—has its own audience, one which demands that subject matter be familiar, that poems contain wit or humor, that language be immediately clear. Writing this kind of poetry is also complicated by the fact that light verse has its own unyielding conventions, a great many of them. The light-verse writer—in conforming to these conventions, in pleasing an audience, and in still writing the poem he intended to write—is a little like the madcap circus juggler. He not only juggles meters, complicated stanza forms, puns, and intricate rhyme patterns; he must simultaneously walk the tight rope of reader appeal.

To initiate the difficulty, there is no definition of "light verse." The term can be used to designate a tremendously wide collection of poetry—most kinds of funny and witty poems, satire, parody, pun, dialect, *vers de société*. A. J. M. Smith considers light verse to be any "poetry at play," but he does not recognize the fact that some people distinguish between poetry (serious) and verse (light). He considers light verse to be poetry, a special kind of poetry—in fact, poetry with a particular difficulty. The technical "virtuosity" which the best light verse demonstrates is also the result of "playfulness," of the intellect at play.[2]

Whatever the formal categories, light verse usually has two qualities in common. First, it is aimed at an audience; or so its subject matter, style, and conversational tone indicate. Light

27

verse must communicate accurately; it must also communicate instantly. Readers do not ponder light verse; they scan it. Most of today's markets for light verse have titles which indicate the necessity of a quick point: the "Parting Shots" page of the *American Legion Magazine*; the "Pepper and Salt" column of the *Wall Street Journal*.

Second, the best light verse is highly polished technically, so polished that the average reader is probably unaware of its technical subtleties. Stanza forms range from the couplet to the sixteenth-century French *rondeau*. In nearly all light verse, every line rhymes somehow, somewhere. Not only must the light-verse poet maintain a regular stanza and definite rhyme and rhythm patterns, he must write in clear, conversational language—and end with his best line, for punch.

This stanza from A. P. Herbert's "I Can't Think What He Sees in Her" evinces the heavy reliance on conversational idiom— which Herbert has italicized—while the poem conforms to a very definite rhyme and rhythm pattern:

> I'm not a jealous woman,
> But *I can't see what he sees in her,*
> *I can't see what he sees in her,*
> *I can't see what he sees in her!*
> If she was something striking
> I could understand the liking,
> And I wouldn't have a word to say to that;
> But I can't see why he's fond
> Of that objectionable blonde—
> That fluffy little, stuffy little, flashy little,
> trashy little, creepy-crawly, music-hally, horrid
> little CAT![3]

The assumedly reasonable opening, "Jealousy's an awful thing," followed by the quick denial—"and foreign to my nature"— creates an effect which is emphatically and intentionally lost in the italicized refrain. That Herbert repeats "I can't see what he sees in her!" three times cannot help but bring home the point. From then on, only the clever rhymes save the poem from redundancy. The break from the couplet rhyme pattern (lines 11 through 16) is refreshing, as is the change in the list of adjectives ("creepy crawly, music-hally" in the catalogue of *little's*).

McGinley often makes use of an imagined conversation that breaks into the poem, either as a refrain ("I wish I didn't talk so much at parties") or as an interruption to the regular stanza and rhythm pattern which—in any long poem—may tend to become oppressive. In "Reactionary Essay on Applied Science," her stanza is a regular sexain (*ababcc*, iambic tetrameter). The interest of the poem lies chiefly in the "spoken" lines that follow each formal stanza:

> I cannot love the Brothers Wright.
> Marconi wins my mixed devotion.
> Had no one yet discovered Flight
> Or set the air waves in commotion,
> Life would, I think, have been as well.
> That also goes for A. G. Bell.
>
> *What I'm really thankful for, when I'm cleaning up after lunch,*
> *Is the invention of waxed paper.*
>
> (96)

Because light verse is usually so regular in form, deviations from that regularity, when they are effective ones, are striking. Ogden Nash has made his name in the light-verse field through his clever manipulations of the irregular. Most light verse contains exact end rhymes, so Nash writes: "I would live all my life in nonchalance and insouciance/ Were it not for making a living which is rather a nouciance.[4] Changing the spelling is also one of Nash's characteristic practices; wild coupling or fusing is another, as is shown by his answer to Dorothy Parker's "Men seldom make passes at girls who wear glasses":

> A girl who is bespectacled,
> She may not get her necktacled;
> But safety pins and bassinets
> Await the girl who fassinets.[5]

Another "irregularity" on which Nash capitalizes is the use of uneven lines, as in "The Evening Out":

> And so goes ten minutes, and then fifteen minutes, and then half an
>   hour,
> And you listen for the sound of water running because you suspect
>   she may have gone back for a bath or a shower,
> Or maybe she is taking a nap,
> Or possibly getting up a subscription for the benefit of the
>   children of the mouse that she said mean things about
>   last night but she is now sorry got caught in a trap, . . .[6]

I digress here for a minute because Nash is known for his clever divergencies from the usual form: most light verse is built on those regular forms.

We have seen how expertly McGinley practices the French *rondeau*. Quatrain, couplet, and sexain—the major forms of light verse—come easily to her, as does the sonnet, a less common structure in light verse. Increasingly in her poetry, McGinley experiments with the more difficult stanza patterns, as "Triolet Against Sisters" shows:

> Sisters are always drying their hair,
>   Locked into rooms, alone,
> They pose at the mirror, shoulders bare,
> Trying this way and that their hair,
> Or fly importunate down the stair
>   To answer a telephone.
> Sisters are always drying their hair,
>   Locked into rooms, alone.

(43)

Obviously, the triolet demands proficiency with rhyme, for only two rhymes—*ABaAabAB*—are used in the eight-line stanza. Skill is necessary to keep the poem from merely repeating itself and to make the reoccurring sounds seem natural.

Another technique of the best light-verse writers is the use of alliteration and assonance. McGinley's beautiful "Legend of the Holly" contains this passage:

> Whiter than shells along the shore
> It blooms on its tree by a stable door.
>
> Villagers come there, half-afraid,
> Gifts in their hands for Child and Maid.[7]

The *s* dominates the quiet poem, slowing it as it sounds both initially and within words. The long vowels (*i* in *whiter*, *o* in *shore*, *e* in *tree*) and the one-syllable words also slow the poem to a stately pace which corresponds well to the content of the passage.

In a much different mood, with the added interest of parody, is John Updike's poem to Helen Traubel, "I Like to Sing Also." Miss Traubel was quoted in *Life* as saying she liked to sing, cook, watch ball games, go to zoos, or read *Life* in the same way she liked to sing. Updike begins after a prose quotation:

> Traubel, Traubel, boil and bubble,
> Gobble fish and cheer a double,
> Warble nobly, ogle cages,
> Wallow deep in *Life's* dark pages.

And in a later refrain,

> Trauble, Trauble, boil and bubble
> Eye of newt and burdock stubble,
> Stir it, burn it, serve with smile;
> *The Valkyries* can vait a vhile.[8]

The last line quoted, as well as the long *o* sound in "Warble nobly, ogle cages" and the long vowels throughout, indicates that Updike also knows the value of assonance and consonance.

These lines from W. S. Gilbert's "Sir Roderic's Song" show an older tradition of sound in light verse, that of rhyme within the line, interior rhyme. Here it serves a dramatic purpose as well as a metrical one:

> As the sob of the breeze sweeps over the trees, and the
>   mists lie low on the fen,
> From grey tombstones are gathered the bones that
>   once were women and men,
> And away they go, with a mop and a mow, to the revel
>   that ends too soon,
> For cockcrow limits our holiday—the dead of the
>   night's high-noon![9]

David McCord makes good use of alliteration in "The Lacquer Liquor Locker" which tells the sad tale of the liquor lackey who threw away the key to the locked, lacquer, liquor, locker. "Not magic of the magi nor the wisdom of the wise" could find a key in time. The king died, and too "the little lackey lastly fell into a deep decline."[10] The epitome of alliteration is Alaric A. Watt's "An Austrain Army" in which each letter of the alphabet dominates sequential lines:

> An Austrian army awfully array'd,
> Boldly by battery beseiged Belgrade.
> Cossack commanders cannonading come
> Dealing destruction's devastating doom. . . .[11]

The writer of light verse usually aims for conciseness. Helpful in pointing to the gist of the poem and in creating ambiguities which may be humorous is an apt title. We have seen how effective McGinley's title "The Adversary" is. Her poem about her shoeless daughters ("girls of sixteen won't keep their shoes on") is entitled "Bootless Speculations." "Collector's Items" heads a poem about the junk to be had for cereal boxtops. One of her best titles, in the sense of purposeful ambiguity, is "Ballade of

Lost Objects." The poem begins: "Where are the ribbons I tie my hair with?/ Where is my lipstick? Where are my hose—" Ostensibly the title refers to the lost *things,* but later the poem centers on the poet's lost children, children who have become women, or as the refrain puts it, "Where in the world did the children vanish?" (52)

As much a part of conventional light verse as the short, rich title is the punch line. These are particularly effective in shorter poems, as these lines from McGinley's "My Own Baedeker" illustrate.

> Although assembled of various famous styles,
> And one of the vastest in all of the British Isles,
> Ely, whenever it rains,
> Makes one aware of the drains—
> For the Master Builders, while certainly up and coming,
> Didn't understand plumbing.
>
> ("Ely," 64)

Although McGinley does not use such a line frequently, one of the most common kinds of punch line is the reversal of intent, as seen in F. P. Adams's "The Rich Man":

> The rich man has his motor-car,
> His country and his town estate.
> He smokes a fifty-cent cigar
> And jeers at Fate.
>
> He frivols through the livelong day,
> He knows not Poverty, her pinch.
> His lot seems light, his heart seems gay,
> He has a cinch.
>
> Yet though my lamp burns low and dim
> Though I must slave for livelihood—
> Think you that I would change with him?
> You bet I would![12]

II *An Attempt at Division*

Although Adams's poem is frequently quoted and often included in anthologies, it seems to me to be an elementary kind of light verse. I would place it in the first level of light verse, if I may divide the great mass of poetry so labeled. "The Rich Man" obeys the conventions of quatrain and iambic measure; it has a punch line; but it has very little else—no particularly good phrases, no striking imagery. Its theme is appropriate to *vers de société*. Adams mockingly criticizes a social type; he makes a point—that condemnation often stems from envy. The poem is more than just foolishness, yet it does not have the "technical virtuosity" that A. J. M. Smith prizes. Perhaps it is too reminiscent of E. A. Robinson; perhaps its language is dated. Other examples of rather undistinguished light verse include most of the quatrains and couplets in the field, forms in which there is not space enough to do more than make a simple statement, as does Richard Armour's "Not a Cloud in the Sky":

> The Indians chant and dance about
> To break a crop-destroying drought,
> But I've a simpler means by far:
> I only have to wash my car.[13]

The limerick, according to both its nature and its form, can create little but simple humor. The clerihew is even more rigidly bound to its conventions.[14] This kind of light verse I would label Level I: the light poem at its simplest, technically.

Level II would include the many kinds of verbal experimentation talked about in the last few pages—intricate stanza forms, wide effects with assonance or alliteration, polysyllabic rhyme. The verbal skill should be evident, even if the poet is indulging himself purely for fun. I think here of David McCord's "History of Education" or his "The Axolotl" ("The axolotl/ Looks a littl/ like the ozolotl,/ Itl// Drink a greatl/ more than whatl/ Fill the fatl/ Whiskey bottl . . .") or of Corey Ford's "The Up-Set" (the battle between "Kid" March and Robert "Farmer" Frost). McGinley has contributed at least one poem to this level, her 1934 "The Garrulous Banana Man" which includes such coined words as *banangular, bananimation, bananimal, bananswer*:

> Have you ever met the Banana Man
> Who drives about with an ancient van,
> In a scarecrow hat and a couple of coats,
> Dispensing fruit and bananecdotes?[15]

This category might be the one in which to place *parody*, a form less popular now than throughout history. The parodist must use his words cleverly, but he remains a mimic rather than an originator.

> Two blind mice
> See how they run!
> They each ran out of the lab with an oath,

For the scientist's wife had injected them both.
Did you ever see such a neat little growth
On two blind mice?[16]

These writers of parody and word play have not failed, of
course, so far as their aims are concerned. But there are greater
light verses. Most readers feel that poetry needs more than a
clever last line to be representative of the best in the human
spirit. Roy Harvey Pearce puts it better when he says that many
people who write light verse have the "sensibility of the least
common denominator—common sense drained of its portion
of *communitas.*" Many light verse writers claim descent from
Andrew Marvell and Robert Herrick, but Herrick's wit, Pearce
feels, is far from the "jokersterism" of some light versifiers.[17]

Perhaps poems like Samuel Hoffenstein's "Poems in Praise of
Practically Nothing" or A. P. Herbert's "At the Theater" indicate
another level of communication—social commentary with greater
technical prowess than the poems dismissed in Level I and with
greater import than those commended in Level II. Herbert's poem
is good, I think, because of its consistently understated tone, as
evident in these lines:

Dear Madam, you have seen this play;
I never saw it till today.
You know the details of the plot,
But, let me tell you, I do not.
The author seeks to keep from me
The murderer's identity,
And you are not a friend of his
If you keep shouting who it is. . . .[18]

"I understand," "I infer"—Herbert's self-deprecation in his exag-
gerated politeness is coolly funny. The poem moves easily in
iambic tetrameter couplets; the rhyme is unobtrusive.

Hoffenstein's "Poems in Praise of Practically Nothing" shows
a bit more originality in rhyme, but the tone of this sequence is
much rougher than Herbert's. Although modern light verse need
not be phrased with the "delicacy" of the original light poems—
those of Anachreon and Horace; of the sixteenth-century lyricists,
the seventeenth-century Cavalier poets, and the eighteenth-
century satirists—still, Hoffenstein's abruptness is far from
polished:

You practice every possible virtue;
You hurt not a soul while others hurt you;

You fetch and carry like a market basket;
What thanks do you get for it? Me don't ask it!

You leap out of bed; you start to get ready;
You dress and you dress till you feel unsteady;
Hours go by, and you're still busy
Putting on clothes, till your brain is dizzy.

Do you flinch, do you quit, do you go out naked?
The least little button, you don't forsake it.
What thanks do you get? Well, for all this mess, yet
When night comes around you've got to undress yet.[19]

A very different poem from Herbert's, but it is appropriate to place it in a Level III classification: reasonable technical proficiency, and an interest in one's world a little beyond pure fun or self-gratification. Phyllis McGinley's "Incident in the Afternoon" (which bears some similarity to Herbert's "At the Theater") is one of the best of this type of poem:

The lights went down. The stage was set.
    Still, in the dusk that fans the senses,
Those ladies I had never met
    Poured out their swollen confidences.
The dialogue was smart. It stirred them
To conversation. And I heard them.
. . . .
They laid their lives, like open tomes,
    Upon my lap and turned the pages.
I heard their taste in hats and homes,
    Their politics, but not their ages.
So much I heard of strange and true
Almost it reconciled me to
One fact, unseemly to recall:
I did not hear the play at all.

(153)

A good poem technically, it is not the best light verse written because it fails thematically.McGinley's final point—that she did not hear the play at all—is the obvious result of the chattering behind her. A wider point is, perhaps, implied in her wry handling of the various matters of gossip, but it is not stated. The sexains are well constructed; rhythms—thanks to short sentences within the lines—are not boring. The failure of "Incident in the Afternoon" is not its technique, but the implication of its theme.

W. H. Auden, who has written some excellent light verse, describes the mode in this way: "There is a certain way of writing which one calls light, but underneath it can carry a great depth of emotion."[20] Level IV of light verse, I think, contains the poems that fit Auden's definition: those that "carry a great weight of emotion" and do it well. McGinley's "The Doll House" is one; her "Dido of Tunisia" is another, a poem which in its theme of war has both an advantage and a disadvantage. There is a great amount of trash written during any period of national conflict; a few of McGinley's poems from the 1940's succumb to excessive emotion, but most show the careful balance of "Dido" (see p. 59).

> I had heard of these things before—of chariots rumbling
>   Through desolate streets, of the battle cries and the danger,
> And the flames rising up, and the walls of the houses crumbling.
>   It was told to me by a stranger.
>
> But it was for love of the fair and long-robed Helen,
>   The stranger said (his name still troubles my sleep),
> That they came to the windy town he used to dwell in,
>   Over the wine-dark deep.
>
> In the hollow ships they came, though the cost was dear.
>   And the towers toppled, the heroes were slain without pity.
> But whose white arms have beckoned these armies here
>   To trample my wasted city?
>
> Ah, this, Aeneas, you did not tell me of:
> That men might struggle and fall, and not for love.
>
>   (110)

The quiet restraint of the Shakespearean sonnet lends dignity to Dido's reminiscence, passive because she had only heard of war. She had not experienced it. Now she has. She puzzles, as the closing couplet recounts: whose love brought armies to Tunisia? No love—men are not falling because of love. McGinley's sad irony is more effective than any vindictive poem could be against the senselessness of war.

Perhaps her "Letter from a Country Inn" is a more representative poem since its subject is less charged emotionally. The simple quatrains with alternately rhyming lines describe the cool rural summer:

> Dinner's at one. They ring an outside gong
> To summon cottagers from down the hill.
> The blue, anonymous days are seasons long,
> And nights derisive with a whippoorwill.

Then the poem turns to a picture of the women, alone, experiencing time which swings "idly as a toy balloon,/ Empty of struggle, almost of thought itself." Here again, McGinley's perceptive view gives us the separateness of two worlds, that of the leisurely woman and that of the hurried man:

> Only at week's end does the tempo vary.
> Then dreaming women rouse themselves from dream,
>
> Tie ribbons in their hair with rapt attention,
> Discard their knitting, put their novels down,
> And half-delighted, half with apprehension,
> Await the train that carries up from town
>
> Their stranger husbands, fetching even here
> Reality's outrageous atmosphere.
>
> (190-91)

A doll house, war, summer in the country—a weight of emotion? technical excellence? Yes. Theme brings with it no guarantee of impact, of significance. Often, poems "about" the most central issues of life are nothing but doggerel—precisely because emotion runs away with the poet as he writes, or because his language is trite. But a combination of technical prowess with theme, with subject matter than has room to wander, room to reach the truly common areas of humanity—this combination frequently creates an excellent poem.

III *In Contrast: Serious Poetry*

We might question placing "The Doll House" and "Dido of Tunisia" in a light-verse category. The newest of serious modern poetry is colloquial. The avant-garde of Charles Olson, Allen Ginsberg, and Robert Creeley; the more established styles of Richard Wilbur, W. D. Snodgrass, Robert Lowell, and James Dickey—nearly all contemporary poetry is lyric. It begins in a personal experience, focuses upon the poet and his reactions to life, and is content with fragments of experience instead of the whole, neat (and often false) picture.

Robert Creeley's quatrain, "I Keep to Myself Such Measures as I Care For," is a free-form lyric:

> I keep to myself such
> measures as I care for,
> daily the rocks
> accumulate position.[21]

The personal point of view is evident as is the incompleteness of the poet's expression. We catch a glimpse of the core of feeling; but we are told too little to either accept or reject that feeling. Regular rhyme and rhythm have been distilled to the sharp simplicity of statement. In two respects, then, this poem differs from the modern light verse of Level IV: (1) it does away with traditional *patterned* conventions like end rhyme and accented rhythm; and (2) it does not recount a complete experience, a complete thought, but only a fragment of emotion. I suppose, in a way, this second point is largely a matter of perspective. The writer of light verse assumes either a third- or a first-person point of view; he often creates a *persona* to serve as narrator of his poem. The *I* or *he* has one reason for being in the poem: to make clear to the reader—using what humor, insight, or didacticism is necessary—the circumstances for the poem. Often, the circumstances *are* the poem ("At the Theater," "The Doll House," etc.). As Paul Bennett maintains, "All poetry is occasional poetry."[22]

The writer of much modern serious poetry, on the other hand, feels no obligation to make the circumstances of a poem clear to his reader. He simply re-creates what has been for him the essence of the moment; in effect, he demands that the reader become a part of his consciousness. As Thomas Parkinson has recently said, modern poetry almost requires that the reader know the poet—know his opinions, his attitudes, his life and circumstances—because of the intensely personal nature of the lyrics being written.[23]

"September 1961" by Denise Levertov illustrates another difference between modern light verse and modern serious verse:

> This is the year the old ones,
> the old great ones
> leave us alone on the road.
>
> The road leads to the sea.

We have the words in our pockets,
obscure directions. The old ones

have taken away the light of their presence,
we see it moving away over a hill
off to one side.

They are not dying,
they are withdrawn
into a painful privacy

learning to live without words.
E. P. "It looks like dying"—Williams: "I can't
describe to you what has been

happening to me"—
H. D. "unable to speak."
The darkness

twists itself in the wind, the stars
are small, the horizon
ringed with confused urban light-haze. . . .[24]

Form is the first, most apparent difference again, as Levertov
writes in what she terms "organic form"—lines and stanzas deter-
mined by the sound and tempo of the individual words. Some of
the lines fall naturally into grammatical phrases—"This is the
year the old ones/ the old great ones/ leave us alone on the
road." Other lines, particularly those later in the poem, are
run-on; and the reader is compelled to read more rapidly. The
subject of the sentence (*darkness, stars, horizon*) needs com-
pleting (*twists, are, ringed*). Consequently, the three images in
these lines are united.

The language and form of even this portion of "September
1961" reflect Levertov's stately, reflective mode. Serious modern
poets view form and language as means of achieving total poetic
effect, not as being important requirements in themselves. The
modern poet does not try to write a sonnet; he attempts to capture
some emotion in words. If the poem moves into a sonnet pattern,
well and good; but form is a secondary consideration, an exped-
ient. (This approach to form is, of course, not new; nor is it
limited to writers of serious poetry.) At any rate, freedom from
prescribed forms has made possible rhythms in poetry which
are more characteristic of the individual poet.

These free form lines from Robert Lowell's "Christmas Eve under Hooker's Statue"

> Tonight a blackout. Twenty years ago
> I hung my stocking on the tree, and hell's
> Serpent entwined the apple in the toe
> To sting the child with knowledge . . .[25]

move very differently from these by Allen Ginsberg ("A Supermarket in California"):

> What thoughts I have of you tonight, Walt Whitman, for
> I walked down the sidestreets under the trees with a headache
> self-conscious looking at the full moon.
> In my hungry fatigue, and shopping for images, I went
> into the neon fruit supermarket, dreaming of your enumerations![26]

At times, the free forms created from the necessity of the poet's expression are, however, as uniform in their own fashion as any traditional pattern. William Carlos Williams, for example, uses a free-form tercet in his understatement of man's essential separateness:

> The metal smokestack
> of my neighbor's chimney
> greets me among the new leaves
>
> it is a small house
> adjacent to my bigger one
> I have come in 3 years
>
> to know much of her
> an old lady as I am an old man
> we greet each other
>
> across the hedge
> my wife gives her flowers
> we have never visited each other[27]

Despite the lack of capitalization and punctuation, William's poem is easy to follow because of its meaningful line division and its cryptic language. There is sadness, but no self-pity. The poet succeeds in showing his emotion rather than telling about it, a technique which enables the reader to re-create his own experience from the poem. Not far from McGinley's technique of listing is William's use of the factual details (*metal smokestack, moon, small house*). The stark description is of value because it creates a mood of objectivity, and it makes the personal comment to come seem more "real."

In retrospect, then, after this very brief look at contemporary serious poetry, we may note several essential differences. First, there is completeness of experience presented in light verse: the serious poet often depends on a slight fragment of happening. He presents the emotion without giving the answers, although they are sometimes implied. Second, the attitude of the *persona*: light verse will probably be written from a more easily perceived point of view. Third, the use of a non-traditional free form in the serious poetry, with a general avoidance of regular rhyme or rhythm.

Obviously, too, there are many similarities between the best light verse and serious poetry. The first is the use of idiomatic, natural speech in both types. The second is a concern with life's meaningful experiences as subjects for poetry—meaningful at least to the poet. The third is the use of the most highly valued poetic devices—metaphor, assonance, alliteration (in moderation).

To some readers, the dividing line between light and serious poetry may seem nebulous. If McGinley had written "The Doll House" without rhyme, would she have had a "serious" poem? The issue is hardly so simple, but perhaps the difference between light and serious work is not so great as some critics would have us believe. As McGinley herself said in 1960, "It wasn't until Wordsworth that there was this great dividing line between 'serious' poetry and 'light verse'."[28] And in 1954 she had explained, "What I have been consciously trying to do recently—ever since I've had enough confidence to consider myself a poet—is to narrow the gulf between 'light' and 'serious' verse. One other thing: I always try to share with my readers the immediacy of my own delight or despair of the world as I see it through my window."[29]

IV *Line of Descent*

David McCord is the only critic I have found who has tried to trace the origins of Miss McGinley's poetry. Most readers and critics take the position of W. H. Auden, who says in his introduction to *Times Three*: "I start a sentence: 'The poetry of Phyllis McGinley is . . .,' and there I stick, for all I wish to say is '. . . is the poetry of Phyllis McGinley.'"[30] Auden would rather compare McGinley with such expert ladies of literature as Marianne Moore, Jane Austen, Virginia Woolf. Unfortunately, he has not the space to explain why—except that they all utilize

well their indefatigable feminine perceptions. So far as literary
technique is concerned, Mr. Auden begs the question; but
McCord takes the plunge. He states that Miss McGinley's work
is modeled after that of Samuel Hoffenstein, Dorothy Parker,
and A. P. Herbert.[31] Herbert, perhaps; but Hoffenstein is much
too rough in his language, stance, and poetic forms to be compared with McGinley. And the only basis for linking Parker and
McGinley is their sex. Miss Parker writes very short poems and
very negative ones. McGinley could never have written "Résumé":

> Razors pain you;
> Rivers are damp;
> Acids stain you;
> And drugs cause cramp.
> Guns aren't lawful;
> Nooses give;
> Gas smells awful;
> You might as well live.[32]

or even the milder "Unfortunate Coincidence":

> By the time you swear you're his,
> Shivering and sighing,
> And he vows his passion is
> Infinite, undying—
> Lady, make a note of this:
> One of you is lying.[33]

McGinley can be sharp in her criticism, yes, but her outlook is
basically optimistic. She admires man; bitterness alone is seldom
in her observations.

Of the three poets McCord has chosen to align with McGinley,
A. P. Herbert is probably the closest. Herbert's forte is poking
gentle fun at a person's weakness; his technical contribution to
light verse seems to be the heavily rhythmic colloquial refrain—
"I can't think what he sees in her"; "I've got the giggles today"
—and McGinley has written several poems of this type. Her
general outlook, also, is similar to Herbert's, although she treats
many more kinds of subjects than Herbert did in his writing
career. Technically, McGinley's poetry is more varied than his.
Still, the comparison is apt so long as it is qualified.

Comparing one poet with another is nearly always fruitless.
Writers are individuals: the differences between them are numer-
ous—and tracing "influences" is tenuous. The practice does have
some validity, however, in a general sense, because poets are

not usually isolated from the work of their fellow poets: they will have some strains in common. Frequently the concept of "school" grows up—the idea that groups of poets are guided by the same artistic principles, and that, consequently, their writing has more likenesses than does a random sampling of poetry.

Categorization is less helpful in discussing light-verse writers because there are so few good poets in that category today. McGinley stands pretty much alone, for these and other reasons. Technically, her poems are extremely sophisticated in their variety of forms and effects. Thematically, too, McGinley's writing is more ambiguous, more subtle, than that of many light-verse writers, aiming as she does not for the merely funny but for the most perceptive insight possible.

McGinley has herself stated that she is trying to write "something a little different—poetry of wit, which is what the Cavalier poets used to write."[34] We might ask, are *wit* and *perception* synonymous? Does wit include the warmth that infuses many of McGinley's poems? T. S. Eliot, in his discussion of Andrew Marvell's "To His Coy Mistress," defines wit as "a tough reasonableness beneath the slight [unostentatious] lyric grace" by which the seriousness of the poem is intensified.[35] Lyric grace, seriousness, wit—no mention of humor per se. In a recent article by Sara Henderson Hay, many good distinctions are drawn between *wit* and *humor*:

> There are nice distinctions between humor and wit, between what is simple playful gaiety and what is veiled or barbed mockery. Wit is to a kind of wisdom—it comes from the German *wissen*—to know—; humor is a matter of high spirits, of pleasant foolery. Wit is brilliant, humor a gentle glow; where wit is incisive and pointed, humor is broad. To pursue it farther, humor is genial, indulgent, well-intentioned; wit is dry, cutting, frequently far from kind.[36]

Considering these informal definitions, and McGinley's poetry in light of them, it is fair to say that Miss McGinley writes from both impulses—incisive wisdom and pleasant foolery. The poems which result are varied, as we have seen. McGinley as poet shares the same distinction she carries as a person—she is complete; her personality has many sides, some parts of which are bound to be contradictory. And, as a poet, she writes not only iambic tetrameter quatrains. Regardless of form, hers is an accomplished poetry.

CHAPTER 3

Amid Incredible Brightness

I *Beginnings*

M cGINLEY'S first books—*On the Contrary* (1934) and *One More Manhattan* (1937)—appeared while the United States was still in the throes of the Great Depression. The effects of that economic catastrophe are evident in some of her poems, but more often McGinley comments obliquely on social inequalities. Her moving "Trinity Place" (p. 55) vividly contrasts starving men and fat pigeons; her sonnet "Love in the Depression" describes the difficulties of love for "the luckless brood, this generation's litter"

> . . . who see their love's good metal
> Moment by moment darken to their gaze
> In the dank air of these corroding days.
>   (270)

Poems more representative of McGinley's attitudes during these years, however, are "The Kingdom and the Glory," "Apostrophe to a Nephew," "The Further Off from England," and "Message from Mars." These poems ridicule the commonplace preoccupations of a nation—and a world—in which thousands were going hungry and as many thousands were being crushed by fascism. People went about their mundane concerns, thinking them "questions so profound." Europe argued over Grace Moore's curtsy to the Dutchess of Windsor, and watched with interest the journeys of baby Lance Reventlow, the Woolworth heir, traveling with, as McGinley phrased it, "hencemen and footmen and handmaidens three" ("And some fear the Fascists and some dread the Debt,/ But Lance goes smiling in his bassinet").

In her 1960 selected poems, *Times Three*, McGinley has grouped these poems of social commentary under the title "The Threadbare Years." At first glance, we relate the title to the

Depression; but, again, this title seems to be ambiguity at its best. Most of the poems in the section deal not with the economics of the world so much as with its morals. The tender "Apostrophe to a Nephew" comments on an adult culture in which "a little child shall feed them," the years of the burlesque baby contests and of adoration for Shirley Temple and her peers. The brilliant "Carol with Variation, 1936" speaks of a world shrouded in armaments, "While brother shoots his brother down, and nation scowls at nation." "Message from Mars" confronts a Fascist Italian editor with his statement that "Culture is necessary but . . . not too much of it." Most of the poems in this group include epigraphs or quotations from daily newspapers. Their inclusion substantiates McGinley's irony: the world is like this; these things do occur.

What Miss McGinley does with these fragments of life is also interesting. She does not rant or rave. She very neatly deflates the hypocritical—as in "Wrong Formula." Irony appears to expert advantage in "Millennium." And she works with all her poetic art to emphasize the moral tragedy of war in "Carol with Variations, 1936." The poem is written in the rhythms of a number of familiar Christmas carols. Some of the lines proper are taken from the traditional songs:

> Oh! Little town of Bethlehem, how still we see thee lie;
> Your flocks are folded in to sleep, and sleep your little ones.
> Behold, there is a Star again that climbs the eastern sky.
> And seven million living men are picking up their guns.

> Hark, the happy cannons roar—
> Glory to the Dictator,
> Death and fear, and peace defiled,
> And a world unreconciled!
>
> (282)

Another stanza begins "God rest you merry, gentlemen, whose will these armies are." The poem concludes in a long catalogue of imperatives, some lines of which are quoted here:

> Sing hosanna, sing Noel.
> Sing the gunner and the shell
> . . . .
> Sing the barbed and bitter wire,
> Poison gas and liquid fire,
> Bullet, bomb, and hand grenade,
> And the heart of man, afraid.

> Christ is come, the Light hath risen,
> All our foes are safe in prison,
> And the Christmastide begets
> Seven million bayonets.
>
> Hear the carol, once again—
> Peace on earth, good will to men.

The fundamental irony of the poem is McGinley's use of the forms and rhythms of the carols themselves and the usual association with love and joy subverted into that of arms, violence, war.

Miss McGinley has made the comment that her poetry has changed with the years, that in the beginning she wrote light—"really light"—verse.[1] The remark needs a little qualification. For McGinley's standards of poetry, perhaps some of the poems from the late 1920's and 1930's are inferior to her later poems. There are some important technical differences between the poems of the 1930's and those of the 1950's—at least among some of them. But, thematically, a survey of the poems included in McGinley's first two books—*On the Contrary* (1934) and *One More Manhattan* (1937)—and many from the third book, *A Pocketful of Wry* (1940), shows that she is as perverse and as particular as ever. She writes about matters that interest her; and she treats these subjects in her characteristically free way. She does not fear the powers that be, nor does she purposely mock them.

There are, to be sure, some highly topical poems—"Nine Day's Wonder" concerns Mrs. Robert McAdoo's new hair style; "The Pathetic Plights of Polly Pecan" is a satire on beauty aids; "Apology for Amnesia" comments on Addison Sims' memory course; "A Wreath for Mrs. Roosevelt" cheers the First Lady because she de-veiled her hat. These poems are not included in *Times Three* (as many from *On the Contrary* are not), probably because their reference is dated. Even in her first book, however, McGinley has written few of the shallow and imitative poems that frequently pass for light verse. One of the "lightest" of her poems in this book is "Slightly Addled Spring Song" in which the change in women's fashions looms as important as the change in season: "For down the lane carouses/ A daffodil revue,/ And little ruffled blouses/ Bedeck the avenue" (*On the Contrary*, 77).

One reason this poem seems slighter than many of McGinley's late poems might well be the shortness of the lines. Several of what I consider weaker early poems are written in dimeter quatrains, and these poems give the feeling of being too rigidly divided; it seems difficult for the poet to express an idea, or the mood relevant to the idea. These few lines from "The Cat That Turned into a Tiger" illustrate one kind of difficulty:

> Eyes like amber,
> It kept her side.
> But once from slumber
> It leaped and cried
>
> With tiger-whining,
> With snarling, glee.
> Its eyes were shining
> Incredibly
>
> . . . .
>
> Then that, the fawner,
> The much-caressed,
> Sprang upon her
> And ripped her breast . . .
> (*On the Contrary,* 88-89)

The sing-song effect of the abrupt, highly accented lines makes ludicrous what should have been a dramatic climax, "And ripped her breast." The steady beat also gives the word *Incredibly* a strange emphasis. McGinley may also have thought these dozen short-lined poems less than successful: she includes none of them in *Times Three*—and rarely does she use the dimeter quatrain in her later work.

If I seem to place undue importance on what poems are used in *Times Three,* I do so because the selections probably represent what McGinley considers her "best" work, for one reason or another. Many good poems have been omitted from the 1960 volume because, as we have observed, they are dated by virtue of reference to contemporary matters—popular songs ("Mairsey Oats"), news items, names of people who have since passed into general oblivion, situations which no longer exist. One of the best of these somewhat dated poems—and there are, unfortunately, many—is "Tiger, Tiger." According to McGinley's epigraph, this poem was written "upon hearing that the Association for Childhood Education . . . was calling Little Black Sambo an 'undesirable book,' because 'it disseminates racial and religious prejudices' ":

> Little Black Sambo, mind your cues;
> Behave like a wary fella.
> Hold on tight to those purple shoes,
> That beautiful green umbrella.
> Better be careful, better not bungle,
> Strolling soft through this civilized jungle.
> Branches bow
> And the grass is hollowed.
> Don't look now
> But I think you're followed.
> Something's after you, angrier far
> Than even your fabulous tigers are—
> A striped thing with a public cry
> And a hot, fanatical tiger eye,
> That lives in bluster and dwells in storm.
> And one of its names is called Reform.[2]

Self-Righteousness comes in for its appraisal in the next stanza, and the poem closes with a warning to Crusoe, Kipling, Uncle Remus and others—"The Peril stalks./ It will soon have treed 'em."

Some other poems seem to have been omitted from *Times Three* because they are "only adequate." They say what is to be said well but with no particular grace; their stanza form is likely to be an octave or quatrain; their meter is probably iambic tetrameter. In these poems, not subject matter so much as technique seems dated.

In collecting poems from the 1930's in *Times Three*, McGinley groups many of them under the heading of "Personal Remarks." Here are the poet's idiosyncrasies: her dislike of the "steadfast ration of ham" in Southern restaurants; her love of winter and its necessary laziness, of a hot bath, of a good bed; her criticism of "progressive" education, of mechanical "inconveniences"; her admiration for women. Here, too, is found McGinley's characteristic insistence on balance in living. "Letter from a Winter Resort" is one of her many poems which pleasantly but firmly insist on a reasonable order:

> The breeze is soft, the sky is blue,
> The sun's a gold persimmon;
> But how dismaying to the view,
> This wilderness of women!
> (210)

As McGinley concludes later in the poem, "any Eden's incomplete/ With Adam nowhere near it." Firm, too, is her belief that

an open mind, a bit of tolerance, is a necessity. In "Lament for
a Wavering Viewpoint," McGinley's irony takes the same form
as in the funny "Lament of the Normal Child" with its blatant
iambic refrain, "Why wasn't I born a Problem Child/ With a
Complex of my own?" McGinley's vocabulary in this poem is
childlike as well as conversational; her phrasing adds much
reality to the complaint:

> I build with blocks when they give me blocks.
>   When it's busy hour, I labor
>
> ··
> From nine to three
> I develop me.
>   I dance when I'm feeling dancy,
> Or everywhere lay on
> With creaking crayon
>   The colors that suit my fancy.
> But when the commoner tasks are done,
>   Deserted, ignored, I stand. . . .
>
> (214)

The point to be made in most of McGinley's ironic laments is,
obviously, that things are pretty much all right as they are.
Nothing is wrong with a man-woman world as it exists; nothing
is better than being "normal." As McGinley declares in the
chauvinistic "Star-Spangled Ode":

> Now more and evermore
> Dear to my heart is this, my native shore,
> Where Liberty lingers still, and even Hope
> Unvanquished dwells
>
> ··
> America, America,
>   I call each prospect good—
>
> (277)

A commonplace of literature is that the social critic, the
satirist, is a person who cares deeply about the state of affairs
which he attacks, perhaps more deeply than his complacent
brothers. The critic is also probably a quixotic optimist whose
expectations are seldom met—consequently, he lives in a state
of chronic disappointment (McGinley's poem "Against Hope"
might be relevant here). I think McGinley's love of her world is
evident throughout her writing in many of her poems. One of the
poems which most freshly expresses her joy in life is her parody

"Intimations of Mortality," written "on being told by the dentist that 'this will be over soon' ":

Indeed, it will soon be over, I shall be done
  With the querulous drill, the forceps, the clove-smelling cotton.
I can go forth into fresher air, into sun,
  This narrow anguish forgotten.

In twenty minutes or forty or half an hour,
  I shall be easy, and proud of my hard-got gold.
But your apple of comfort is eaten by worms, and sour.
  Your consolation is cold.

This will not last, and the day will be pleasant after.
  I'll dine tonight with a witty and favorite friend.
No doubt tomorrow I shall rinse my mouth with laughter.
  And also that will end.

The handful of time that I am charily granted
  Will likewise pass, to oblivion duly apprenticed.
Summer will blossom and autumn be faintly enchanted.
  Then time for the grave, or the dentist.

Because you are shrewd, my man, and your hand is clever,
  You must not believe your words have a charm to spell me.
There was never a half of an hour that lasted forever.
  Be quiet. You need not tell me.

                                        (233)

The lightness of the occasion for the poem is restated in every stanza, but is used to particularly good advantage in the third, "I shall rinse my mouth with laughter"; and in the fourth, "time for the grave, or the dentist." Movement within each stanza, however, counteracts the apparent levity. McGinley does not attempt to follow Wordsworth's stanzaic pattern; she uses quatrains of iambic pentameter, with the fourth line written in much slower trimeter—"This narrow anguish forgotten"; "And also that will end." The last stanza captures the poignancy of her admission (built from the fourth one) in its naturally phrased sentences, sentences short with painful resolution: "There was never a half of an hour that lasted forever./ Be quiet. You need not tell me."

I like to couple this poem with some of McGinley's best early writing, "Six Nuns in the Snow." There is no apparent simliarity between these poems except that the second describes the kind of person the speaker in "Intimations" seems to be—candid, calm, loving. Tone and pace are also somewhat the same, but more meditative than in many of McGinley's early poems:

> Beautifully, now, they walk among these new
> petals the snow shook down—
> identical figures, going two by two,
> each in a black gown.
>
> With what a placid tread, what definite,
> calm impulse each proceeds,
> two by two, black on bewildering white,
> swinging her long beads;
>
> an absolute six, taking their candid way
> undazzled by this whiteness,
> who have grown used to walking without dismay
> amid incredible brightness.
>
> (232)

"Six Nuns" is written in syllabic verse, and longer lines of ten or eleven syllables alternate with those of five, six, or seven. Each stanza concludes with a short, slow line; and emphasis is gained through the distinctness of each separate word, "each in a black gown," "swinging her long beads." The sense of a definite ending for each stanza is important because every verse is a thematic unit.

The first stanza very simply introduces the nuns—identical, dressed in black. The snow dominates the picture, however, because of the metaphoric "new petals" and because McGinley opens the poem with its description. In the second stanza, the nuns assume character, although the stanza adds nothing new in a denotative sense: again, the nuns walk in the snow. We know now, however, that they are placid and sure, that they move by definite impulse. We know, too, that the whiteness is "bewildering," at least to the narrator. This subjective detail is important chiefly for the resolution of the last stanza.

From a picture dominated by the snow, McGinley progresses in the third stanza to her metaphoric conclusion—the nuns are superimposed on the dazzling whiteness (the "bewildering" whiteness) of this scene (by which they remain "undazzled") and on a heavenly atmosphere, this one of "incredible brightness." Because of their double environment, so to speak, the nuns are absolute on earth: they can afford to be candid since they "have grown used to walking without dismay."

This poem gives good evidence of McGinley's poetic skills. All three stanzas "say" the same thing, but a clear progression in effect to the end of the poem is achieved. The well-chosen adjective (for example, the omission of *black* in stanza three), the conversational phrase ("Beautifully, now, they walk . . ."), the accumulation of detail as if the poet were, in fact, watching the nuns walk—all obtain the effect of perfect naturalness.

The thematic tie between this poem and "Intimations of Mortality" lies, I think, in the poet's awareness of the nuns' place on earth: evanescent but decidedly happy. "Amid incredible brightness" is another of McGinley's ambiguous references—the nuns' environment resembles heaven, but it is still a part of this earth. The realization that she must leave this unbelievable world saddens the poet of "Intimations." For, to the poet speaking here, this world is very much worth living in.

The titles of two other groups of McGinley's poems from the 1930's, as designated in *Times Three*, help to explain the poet's growing contentment. She now lives in New York—or, at first, in New Rochelle—an area greatly different from the Western country in which she was reared and educated. McGinley loves the city, as her "Valentine for New York" shows: "Tumultous town, absurd and thunderful,/ I think you're wonderful—/ Sleeping or waking, frivolous or stable,/ Down at the heels, or opulent in sable. . . ." From the great reaches of experience to the quiet comforts that are necessary in any person's life—New York has them all; and McGinley was observing, and writing about, most of them. Many of the poems in the section titled "On the Town" are jovial by nature of their rhythm and structure, eight-line stanzas of iambic measure. "Midsummer Mediations" reflects on the mushrooming of outdoor cafes ("Give me a dim interior/ And Let me munch alone./ For I am sick of sidewalks/ Whereon to break my bread"); "Elegy with a Pewter Lining" sings the praises of the Aquacade; "Song from New Rochelle" very nicely states the plight of the commuter:

> Monday's child is fair of face,
>   And her driver's a handsome fellow.
> Tuesday's child is full of grace,
>   So she gracefully hails a Yellow.
> Wednesday's child has a red coupe,
>   With a little black horn she toots.
> But I was born on a Saturday,

And Saturday's child commutes!

CHORUS

No responsibility is assumed for errors in timetables
Nor for inconvenience or damage resulting from delayed trains
Or failure to make connections. . . .

(258)

With good effect, McGinley uses phrases from timetables as her accent "chorus" in this poem: "The schedules shown herein are subject/ To change without notice." She also includes poems with more experimental forms in this collection. There are a number of parodies, for example, as well as the beginning of some characteristic practices: "Heat Wave" is one of the first of McGinley's long-short line quatrains:

These are the days democratic, the days without barriers.
Every man is a brother.
Strangers speak at the stations, at counters. In common carriers
They commiserate with each other. . . .

(241)

The gentle "Ode to Mr. Zimmerman" employs the catalogue, written in iambic lines of varying lengths. It is, however, more than a listing of foods in the corner delicatessen. McGinley is not impressed with the appearance or the taste of these viands; it is their smell that entrances her.

a fragrant place is the corner place
of Mr. Zimmerman's pride.
My nose goes up
Like a terrier pup
Whenever I step inside.
For coffee bubbles behind a screen,
The air is rich and murky,
And the smell to the west is still unguessed
But the northeast smell is turkey.

(239)

As the poet re-emphasizes, "I'm going down to the corner,/ Insouciant as you please,/ To sniff at dishes/ Of pickled fishes/ And little curled anchovies." True to the definition of the Horatian ode as personal, tranquil, and contemplative, McGinley writes this praise of her "constant love/ For the fragrance of/ The corner delicatessen."

The poem is divided into three sections which might be intended to parallel the strophe, antistrophe, and epode of the traditional ode, a form which is marked too by its intricate rhyme pattern. The last can be found easily in "Ode to Mr. Zimmerman." McGinley never writes limericks per se, but the groups of lines early in each of these stanzas are written in near-limerick form, the third and fourth lines being much shorter and rhyming. Each stanza opens and closes with this arrangement, an interesting variation on McGinley's more customary octave form.

The poet's fourth category for her poems of the 1930's is entitled "The House of Oliver Ames." It includes poems written about her husband (she was married to Charles Hayden in 1936) and, more generally, about married life. In this vein of subject matter, McGinley is writing lighter verse than comparable poems from the decades to come. She is touching the superficialities of marriage in "Oliver Meets an Emergency," "A Marriage of Convenience," and "Apology for Husbands," the latter of which concludes:

> What gadget's useful as a spouse?
>   Considering that a minute,
> Confess that every proper house
>   Should have a husband in it.
>
>   (260)

"Don't Write, Wire" is an amusing reading of Oliver's love letters as compared with those of Shelly and other poets; "Recipe for a Marriage," a parody of Robert Burn's "John Anderson My Jo," concludes that husband and wife end up sharing each others' faults instead of virtues. The only tender poem in "The House of Oliver Ames" is the derivative sonnet, "View from a Suburban Window:

> When I consider how my light is spent,
>   Also my sweetness, ditto all my power,
> Papering shelves or saving for the rent. . . .

McGinley's octave describes her days "apprenticed/ Forever to a grinning household muse." The sestet of this sonnet presents the opposite, consoling view:

> And how I might, in some tall town instead,
>   From nine to five be furthering a Career,
>   Dwelling unfettered in my single flat,
> My life my own, likewise my daily bread—
>   When I consider this, it's very clear
>   I might have done much worse. I might, at that.
>
>   (269)

II "*Really Light Verse*"

"View from a Suburban Window" shows clearly that McGinley respects the conventions of the Petrarchan sonnet. When she writes Shakespearean sonnets, the last six lines do not oppose the octave. The third quatrain continues the theme of the poem, and the closing couplet serves as a summary. In even this slight difference of arrangement, McGinley is a meticulous observer of poetic conventions. Technically, the impression of McGinley's poems from the 1930's is that she relies on conventional forms (with occasional parodies of lines within an appropriate form, as in the above poem) or that she makes great use of one- or two-stanza forms which work well for her—the eight-line iambic stanza, or the alternately rhyming quatrain. In addition, McGinley begins experimenting with her own innovations within standard forms—with the long-short alternating line, which she uses on occasion throughout her writing career. Another is the three-line interval in a rhyme pattern, used to break the regular *a a* or *abab* rhyme scheme. A third is her willingness to vary a refrain and to substitute the rhythms of prose for those of poetry in a refrain.

Variation within refrain lines gives power to one of McGinley's strongest early poems. "Trinity Place" is composed of three quatrains, each one of which ends with a comparison of the busy, fat pigeons and the hungry, idle men of Depression years:

The pigeons that peck at the grass in Trinity Churchyard
   Are pompous as bankers. They walk with an air, they preen
Their prosperous feathers. They smugly regard their beauty.
They are plump, they are sleek. It is only the men who are lean.
The pigeons scan with disfavor the men who sit there,
   Listless in sun or shade. The pigeons sidle
Between the gravestones with shrewd, industrious motions.
The pigeons are busy. It is only the men who are idle.
The pigeons sharpen their beaks on the stones, and they waddle
   In dignified search of their proper, their daily bread.
Their eyes are small with contempt for the men on the benches.
It is only the men who are hungry. The pigeons are fed.

                                              (270-71)

McGinley works with a number of techniques in this short poem, but the refrainlike concluding lines summarize and restate each stanza's impression. The first quatrain presents the pigeons, prosperous and proud (and identified at all times with hard, plosive words—*peck, pompous, bankers, preen, prosperous, smugly, plump, sleek*). No mention is made of anything other than the birds until the fourth line, the "refrain": "They are plump, they are sleek. It is only the men who are lean." So quiet are the sibilants here that the comparison goes almost unnoticed. The second stanza, however, elaborates the contrast.

Just as the lean men made their appearance quietly, so they sit, listless. "The pigeons are busy" with "shrewd," industrious motions"—sidling, scanning, searching the gravestones. In another kind of contrast, the men sit idle. Sharp descriptive words continue in stanza three, while the birds' activity—and their contempt for the quiet men—grows. This third line of refrain begins with the description of the men—"hungry." It closes, as the entire poem does, with the pigeons. "Trinity Place" is the pigeons' place; it also is the pigeons' poem: "The pigeons are fed." The men only watch. The pigeons pass judgment, a judgment which the men—spiritless, broken—seem to accept.

There are many good early McGinley poems. Others from the 1930's are good light verse, without achieving what has come to be her usual excellence. Too frequently, McGinley's earlier poems are written in iambic tetrameter, as is "Dissertation on Furniture," with a heavy dependence on catalogues to provide content. Sometimes, of course, the latter can be extremely apt and/or funny, but any device becomes boring when used too often.

Some of McGinley's early poems contain the kind of "slant" rhyme considered legitimate for use in light verse, *Edison* and *medison, raw gust* and *August, luncheon* and *munch on, sandwiches* and *bandwiches.* Usually these rhymes only detract from the total poem, even though they spring from a long, light-verse tradition; McGinley's poem to St. Valentine, "Poor Timing," may serve as an example:

> When winds blow up and snow comes down
>   And the whole gray world seems horrider,
> And every lass that sulks in town
>   Thinks wistfully of Florider,
> Pity the chapped and wintry maid
>   Who'd trade the arms that clasp her in,
> For Vitamin A and a nasal spray
>   And maybe a bottle of aspirin.

(224)

There are also in other of her poems the puns on familiar phrases or lines from well-known poems, "When the dew is on the milk-man and the bacon's on the grill" or "I wandered happy as a cloud/Afloat with fellow-cumuli" or "What's so rare as a day in June/Without a gift to shop for?"

Occasionally, McGinley goes further in her borrowings by adapting lines and forms from a famous poem, as is the case of "Recipe for a Marriage, with a curtsy to Mr. Burns." Although the poem begins with the lines from Burns's "John Anderson My Jo," its theme is quite different; in length, it has thirty-eight lines instead of twenty-four; and only the last stanza ends with Burns's refrain. As McGinley's subtitle indicates, the resemblance is unmistakable, and intentional. She is using the suggestion of the warmest of love poems for her own purposes: an enumeration of faults she and her husband share.

Of all the technical practices of the 1930's, only McGinley's titles seem less than effective: "Lament of the Normal Child," "Ode to the Bath," "Song for an Engraved Invitation," "Dirge over a Pot of Pâté de Foie Grass," "Reflections Outside a Gymnasium," "Ballad of the Lord and Columbus." There are also the titles that suggest the messages, carols, elegies, notes, meditations, apostrophes, recipes, mottoes, lines, letters, dissertations, histories, complaints, apologies, advice. Strangely, although again in the light-verse tradition, McGinley writes no *poems.* Not one of the verses from this decade included in *Times Three* has the word *poem* in its title.

There are several apparent reasons for this method of entitling light verse. The first is the association inherent in a word like *"song"* used as a title. The reader expects some musical qualities in the poem—perhaps a refrain, a strong rhythm, a relatively weak lyric. With designations like "ode" or "dirge," it is possible to satirize the expected form if the poet does not choose to follow its conventions (as McGinley does in her modern "Epithalamion"). Basically, calling his poem something other than a poem seems to be an accepted pose of the light-verse writer. Whether modestly or hypocritically, the poet appears to join the critics who assume that light verse is something other than poetry. It is interesting that McGinley's later poems are not so frequently entitled in this manner.

We might well ignore the comparatively minor reservations I have made in my overview of McGinley's poems from the 1930's. I think her work that has been quoted shows that McGinley's early writing illustrates her consistent verbal skill and her interest in the world about her—its admirable qualities as well as its foibles. For the most part, these are good poems; a great many of them show that McGinley is already beginning to move toward the "incredible brightness" of her later work.

CHAPTER 4

"The World Was Safe for Living"

I *War*

Savor the hour as it comes. Preserve it in amber.
Instruct the mind to cherish its sound and its shape.

SO begins McGinley's moving poem "V-Day," a poem which
captures the spirit of the 1940's, the decade of her writings
with which we are here concerned. Literarily, economically,
politically, and emotionally, the 1940's were dominated by World
War II—rightfully so. And this chapter, too, will be dominated
by McGinley's war poems, for several reasons. First, in the midst
of an incredible amount of bad war poetry—gross, maudlin, overly
sentimental, prejudicial—McGinley managed, on the whole, to
write good poems. She wrote in a variety of attitudes; she wrote
about a wide span of war-related subjects; she wrote "serious"
poems and funny poems—and satiric poems.

Second, and perhaps more important for the central focus
of this study, the artistry of the poet, McGinley's versatile handling of the pervasive theme of war is proof that she can do
whatever she wants, technically, in her poetry:

Safe was the day and the world was safe for living
   For Democracy, Liberty, all of the coin-bright names
. . . .
That was an island in time, secure and candid,
   When we seemed to walk in freedom as in the sun,
With a promise kept, with the dangers of battle ended,
   And the fearful perils of peace not yet begun.

(122)

In "V-Day," McGinley captures the quiet hope of a country still
powerful after a debilitating war, the hope of the people—"the
women kneeling in churches, the people's laughter." Promises
are not yet broken; ideals are still "coin-bright." To express the

59

relative tranquility of this time, she uses a longer line than in many of her poems—a varied iambic pentameter. Characteristic of the pentameter line, many segments fall into two phrases as if they contained a formal caesura. The mood is stately.

McGinley's earlier poem "The Portents" parallels "V-Day" in its dignified solemnity. Moving from the epigraph, "Trial blackout of city studied by officials," McGinley treats the blackout as a portent of things to come: active engagement in the war. The poem, however—somewhat strangely for McGinley—is metaphoric. It deals with "weather" and the coming storm, the "blast" and evanescent personal safety. The poem first describes how "the knowing eye and the reason/ Predict the season":

> By a cloud, by rings on the moon
> Or a bough that casts no shadow,
> By a snowflake falling at noon
> In a shriveled meadow

Already ominous by reason of the shadowless bough and the shriveled meadow, the poem continues with an expression of man's inadequacy. The generally long sentences and smooth rhythms are pulled down in the conclusion. The short, abrupt sentences reflect the poet's discomforting realization—once again, phrased with McGinley's effective understatement:

> Whose hands—not yours, not mine—
> Shall hold the floods in tether?
> We have seen the cloud and the sign,
> But we cannot stay the weather.
> Run to your house. Pull fast
> Your shutters on the blast.
>
> Though there is no safety there,
> I think. Nor anywhere.
>
> (105)

The consistent mood of forboding is established by the ritard in tempo and the strong patterns of assonance used in the first stanza and then sporadically throughout. In this context, the sexain rhyme scheme (*ababcc*) adds to the feeling of finality. Each stanza ends with a closed couplet, as does the poem itself.

Metaphor is again the central device in the ironic "Ballad of Fine Days." This poem is one example of McGinley's use of form for ironic purposes. The lilting ballad stanza is appropriate only to the title, another irony. These are not "fine days," these days of bombing and razing. They are "fine" only in the sense of the most denotative weather report, and McGinley's quotation from a BBC broadcast underlies the fact that even weather is essentially committed to war: "Temperatures have soared to almost summer levels . . . making conditions ideal for bombing offensives":

> All in the summery weather,
>   To east and south and north,
> The bombers fly together
>   And the fighters squire them forth.
>
> (106)

The metaphor occurs in stanzas two and three, when McGinley describes the lilac and the buttercups along with the "fiercer buds" of the bombings: "There blooms tonight in Essen/ What bloomed in Coventry." (McGinley used this figure earlier in "Mr. Browning Revises—1940.")

"The Mixture as Before" shares with the ballad above the irony of form in that McGinley employs her frequent eight-line iambic tetrameter stanza. She tries to create "one soft, deceptive hour" in summer. True to her title, the form is as before; the content is almost as before, except for the touches of ironic description like "the anti-aircraft gun/ Crouches in astonished meadows" and "the aromatic night/ Leans against the blackout curtain."

Another of McGinley's war poems, "Landscape without Figures," is frequently quoted. This poem presents the normal villages ("The shape of the summer has not changed at all") saddened, emptied of the vital young men who "boasted, and swam, and lounged at the drugstore's portal," never thinking "but that they were immortal." The images are reasonably successful, but the poem suffers from a too-long catalogue of the boys' activities. The same complaint might be made about the well-known "Soldier Asleep." Here McGinley describes the dangers the soldier is prey to, contrasted with the safe places of sleep he had known as a civilian ("The double-decker at home, the bench in the park,/ The attic cot, the hammock under the willow"). When compared with the expertly restrained "Dido of Tunisia" (see p. 36), these two poems seem redundant.

Variety in pace gives life to McGinley's group of war poems. She is not afraid to depict real fear; she attempts to re-create the homefront loneliness; but she is not above finding what fun must exist in nearly all human situations. Ironically entitled, in her poem "Horrors of War" form and tempo change once again, to remain in harmony with her subject and attitude toward it:

> Upon this meek civilian head
> There fall few blows I can't put up with.
> I slice my own unbuttered bread
> And creamless coffee fill my cup with.
> To market in my rationed shoes
> I trudge on patient metatarsals,
> Select the reds, tear out the blues,
> And homeward stagger with my parcels.
> 'Tis not the want of morning bacon,
> 'Tis not the storage cupboard bare
> Which cause my life at times to take on
> This aspect of despair.
>
> *It's amateur dieticians*
> *Telling me how to make meat loaf out of peanut butter.*
>
>   (114-15)

Prose choruses again provide excellent contrast to the regular lines of the formal, twelve-line stanzas. The concluding stanza, a quatrain, departs from that regular rhythm, as the last line is extremely long, thanks to a string of appropriate adjectives:

> Let the bomb burst, I shall not fear.
> Let foemen march, I'll guard my city.
> *But none shall force this outraged ear*
> *To listen to another radio crooner warbling another*
>   *alleged patriotic ditty.*

"Ballad of Citations," "Admonition," "Chant of the Optimistic Butcher" (with its mocking refrain, "Variety meats, variety meats,/ Who will buy my variety meats?"), "A Reader's-Eye View of the War," "Fiesta in the Reich"—all express the lighter side of the conflict in regular iambic rhythms and sly rhymes.

Some of McGinley's war poems which she did not include in *Times Three* show, however, a different approach to the conflict. "Old Rhyme" borrows the nursery-rhyme form: "Watch out below/ Cries the great bell at Bow/ You make a fine target/ Say the bells of St. Marg'et." "The Holy City" refers to war measures in Palestine where bugles are to be blown only as signs of danger. The irony that man's hate has silenced even the holy city, is well expressed in the slow quatrains and quinquains:

> Lower your gates, Jerusalem.
> Make mute the sacred horn,
> While dark comes down
> Upon that town
> Wherein the Light was born.
>
> *(Stones,* 153)

It is interesting to note that, whenever McGinley's attention turns to war, she is sympathetic. She never writes against the Nazi cause; she refrains from blame. "Hamburg," for example, shows the pity which the observer feels for the wanton destruction of the city:

> These are the wounds of war, prescribed and legal;
> The eye for the broken eye, the tooth for a tooth,
> The just though merciless blow.
>
> *(Stones,* 162)

This poem expresses the quandary of war: how man can be "just" while being "merciless." McGinley does not supply answers; she only points out that "Gretchen for her children weeps no louder/ Than Rachel wept."

The quatrain with its shorter, slowing fourth line is the same form McGinley uses in the ironic "Homicide Makes the Headlines," a poem which points vividly to the contradiction between the celebrity of one man's murder and the ignominy of hundreds of soldiers' deaths:

> The circumstances, too, are most unusual.
> He was not storming a beach or leading a raid,
> Nor fell in mortar fire nor felt the casual
> Shock of the flung grenade,
>
> But lay at his own door (see page eleven
> For diagrams, details, and picture spread) . . .
>
> *(Stones,* 163)

Another quatrain—this time of the alternating long-short line pattern—is McGinley's "Report on the Town." The poet describes New York in a seemingly casual listing of activities and scenes, with only occasional references to war. Short sentences and the irregular anapestic lines give "Report on the Town" a tone of carefully controlled nostalgia. The poet obviously has her reader (and his memories) in mind:

> It's hard to get tickets for shows. Each fabulous counter
> Yet draws the fabulous throng.

> The busses grind. Prometheus leaps at the Center.
> The casualty lists grow long.
>
> . . . .
>   nobody's starved
> In spite of two "meatless days." We complain of taxes.
> But no bomb falls . . .
>
> (Stones, 160)

Quatrains, couplets, sexains, sonnets—the stanzaic forms are varied as McGinley approaches the subject of war from a number of viewpoints. Despite—or perhaps because of—this assortment of techniques, the body of McGinley's war poetry reflects a dispassioned participant, *participant* because the poet is involved enough to see many facets of the conflict, both military and human. But she is *dispassioned* because she somehow avoids the emotional imbroglio evident in so much poetry from the 1940's.

II   . . . And Peace

Only about one quarter of McGinley's poems written during this decade deal with war, for more of her writing treats what she described in "V-Day" as "an island in time, secure and candid." McGinley's "island," in place, as her 1949 *Harper's* article[1] showed, was the much maligned suburbia; and her "island in time" was her several years as a homemaker with a husband and two small daughters. McGinley's poems from the 1940's are about parades, Halloween, a village in spring, household budgets, Christmas, income tax, her children leaving for school. There is no shadow of war; she describes her village as if it were isolated; she compares it with Arcadia and Camelot. Most of her poems reflect the serenity of the complacent homemaker, but that attitude is coupled with the perspicacity of a sage social observer. Needless to say, the two are not always so joined; for perspicacity does not frequently lead to a contentment.

I think particularly of "The 5:32," a sonnet from McGinley's sequence on suburban living, as exemplifying this tranquil joy in a woman's daily life:

> She said, If tomorrow my world were torn in two,
> Blacked out, dissolved, I think I would remember
> (As if transfixed in unsurrendering amber)
> This hour best of all the hours I knew:
> When cars came backing into the shabby station,

Children scuffing the seats, and the women driving
With ribbons around their hair, and the trains arriving,
And the men getting off with tired but practiced motion.

Yes, I would remember my life like this, she said:
Autumn, the platform red with Virginia creeper,
And a man coming toward me, smiling, the evening paper
Under his arm, and his hat pushed back on his head,
And wood smoke lying like haze on the quiet town,
And dinner waiting, and the sun not yet gone down.

(137)

Because of its resonant letters—*l's, r's, m's, n's*—and its sibilants, the poem reads slowly, as befits its meditative tone; the catalogue of descriptive details is one of the most vivid in McGinley's poetry; and natural phrasing counteracts any austerity the sonnet form might tend to impose. Thanks to McGinley's prowess with this form, "The 5:32" does read like the wife, speaking.

If this poem embodies womanly contentment, "Volunteer Fireman" illustrates a wifely sympathy, and "Occupation: Housewife" denotes another area of McGinley's clear-sightedness. As her prose writing also makes apparent, she recognizes the ambiguities of woman's situation. This portrait of the "encroaching desolation" that a woman faces as her children leave and her life empties is slight but accurate—the competitive spirit, the reminiscence about "what might have been," the immobility, the bridge games. With more variation in technique but with much the same point is "Hostess," a portrait of a woman "desperately bent/ On stirring up a scheduled merriment."

Again, McGinley writes many poems of social criticism during the 1940's—a "brief history of modern man" condensed into the symbol of "Tiptoe, the weathercock"; a tirade against the City of Brotherly Love for refusing to erect a statue of Tom Paine; a critique of modern journalism; critical glances at elections, taxes, and unions. Though probably serious in intent, most of these poems are written in the lilting iambic tetrameter that the poet handles so well; and their rhythm and form makes their denotative impact less harsh.

Compared with McGinley's earliest poems, her work from this period does show innovation. Thematically, she has branched into areas like literary criticism and the Christmas season with its related warmth and foolishness. She has a few very short— almost aphoristic—poems about concepts instead of situations.

These mark a departure in that most of them are written in the short-line quatrain form common to light verse—a form McGinley has seldom used—yet they make no pretense at being "light." "A Choice of Weapons" is one poignant example:

> Sticks and stones are hard on bones.
> Aimed with angry art,
> Words can sting like anything.
> But silence breaks the heart.
>
> (159)

The colloquial phrasing in this quatrain—"like anything," "are hard on"—helps the poem reach the audience immediately. That only the second and fourth lines rhyme also gives the poet more freedom in her word choice. Slight as it is, this deviation from what has been McGinley's norm (of rhyming every line) gives some foreshadowing of the more fluid poems of the 1950's.

One of the strengths of the frequently quoted poem, "Blues for a Melodeon," is McGinley's abrupt swing to an unrhyming dimeter line after three lines of tetrameter (here, first and third rhyming) in each quatrain. The strange, sudden ending of each stanza parallels the poet's own sudden realization—"delicate ruin" has overtaken her home and her person. The odd rhyme pattern only intensifies the starkness of her mood:

> A castor's loose on the buttoned chair—
> The one upholstered in shabby coral.
> I never noticed, before, that tear
> In the dining-room paper.
>
> When did the rocker cease to rock,
> The fringe sag down on the corner sofa?
> All of a sudden the Meissen clock
> Has a cherub missing.
>
> All of a sudden the plaster chips,
> The carpet frays by the morning windows;
> Careless, a rod from the curtain slips,
> And the gilt is tarnished.
>
> This is the house that I knew by heart.
> Everything here seemed sound, immortal.
> When did this delicate ruin start?
> How did the moth come?
>
> Naked by daylight, the paint is airing

Its rags and tatters. There's dust on the mantel.
And who is that gray-haired stranger staring
    Out of my mirror?

                                                    (196)

W. H. Auden comments that this poem illustrates some key differences in the masculine and feminine imagination. Auden says that "the feminine imagination accepts facts and is coolly realistic."[2] As a result, most of McGinley's poems lack "nostalgia." The theme of "Blues," Auden points out, "the passing of youth and the oncome of middle-age, has frequently been treated by men. As a rule, they devote their words to their memories of themselves—once I could fun very fast, once I was admired by the girls, once I was very bright, etc., but now. . . . In Phyllis McGinley's poem, the 'I' does not appear until the last two lines and the past is hardly mentioned."[3]

Innovation is not, of course, the whole story in any poet's maturity. McGinley's body of poems from the 1940's show, too, that her familiar stanza forms still work very successfully. "To a Lady in a Phone Booth," one of her best funny poems, is written in the now-polished iambic tetrameter sexain. The first stanza contains the apostrophe to the lady ("Plump occupant of Number Eight/ Outside whose door I shift my parcels/ And wait and wait and wait and wait/ With aching nerves and metatarsals") and the leading question: "What keeps you sitting in that booth?" Subsequent stanzas pose possible answers to the question:

Say, was the roof above you sold
    By nameless landlord, cruel and craven,
Till, driven by imperious cold,
    You find this nook your only haven?
Yield me the instrument you hoard,
And I will share my bed and board.

. . . .

That paper clutched within your fist—
    I cannot quite make out the heading—
Madam, is that a formal list?
    Do you, by chance, arrange a wedding?
Or—dreadful thought I dare not speak!—
Perhaps you rent here by the week.

                                                    (164)

Exaggeration and anticlimax help keep the poem humorous to its conclusion, as the poet guesses one more time:

Yet, as I totter out of line,
A faint suspicion waxes stronger.
Oh, could it be your feet, like mine,
Would simply bear you up no longer?
So did you happen, unaware,
Upon this cubicle, with chair,

And did it seem in all the town
One spot where you could just sit down?

This poem also illustrates McGinley's use of alternating masculine and feminine rhymes—as she says of the pattern, "a favorite device of mine to create music and avoid monotony."[4]

III New Perspective

In her work during the 1940's, McGinley shows her greatest insight—and the first signs of a real tenderness—in her writing about and for children. Her poem "Here Come the Clowns— Didn't They?" is as funny as "The Velvet Hand" is rueful. McGinley is to write stronger poems about her children as they reach adolescence, but this earlier parent-child relationship comes through vividly in poems like "One Crowded Hour of Glorious Strife." Alternating stanza forms accent the poet's wit: long lines of iambic tetrameter state and restate her love for her children. The stanzas of dimeter rhythm, in contrast, pound away as they list the mother's countless tasks in getting the girls off to school:

I love my daughters with a love unfailing,
I love them healthy and I love them ailing.
I love them as sheep are loved by the shepherd,
With a fiery love like a lion or a leopard.
I love them gentle or inclined to mayhem—
But I love them warmest after eight-thirty a.m.

Oh, the peace like heaven
That wraps me around,
Say, at eight-thirty-seven,
When they're schoolroom-bound
With the last glove mated
And the last scarf tied,
With the pigtail plaited,
With the pincurl dried,
And the egg disparaged,
And the porridge sneered at,

> And last night's comics furtively peered at,
> The coat apprehended
> On its ultimate hook,
> And the cover mended
> On the history book!
>
> How affection swells, how my heart leaps up
> As I sip my coffee from a lonely cup!
> For placid as the purling of woodland waters
> Is a house divested of its morning daughters.
> Sweeter than the song of the lark in the sky
> Are my darlings' voices as they shriek good-by—
> (184)

The contrasting images in the last stanza quoted are particularly effective—the placid house (like *purling woodland waters,* never); the tranquility of the "lonely cup"; and the crowning comparison of the lark's song and the girls' voices "as they shriek good-by."

Remaining stanzas bring in the mention of Cornelia and her children as the jewels of her life. As McGinley concludes her poem, "But Cornelia, even, must have raised three cheers/ At the front door closing on her school-bent dears." One of McGinley's strengths—as poet and as person—is surely this ability to recognize her feelings, and to accept them as natural.

And what about children—hers and those of the world at large? Strange as they may behave at times, children "belong to the human race," she states in her poem, "About Children": "Equipped with consciousness, passions, pulse,/ They even grow up and become adults." There are, to be sure, differences. But the important thing about McGinley's view of children is that in it they are people; they do have "consciousness" and "passions."

Accordingly, McGinley thinks that books for children should be as good as those for adults—perhaps better in that they should have "accomplished style, honest motivation, characters proficiently drawn."[5] Children's books should not be subjected to the "stranglehold" of a preselected vocabulary, and they should be more than picture books (McGinley thinks many are over-illustrated). Most important of all, however, books for children should be based on "genuine emotion." Whether events are fanciful or true is immaterial. The theme, the pervasive tone, is the significant impression; for these books, McGinley feels, are "the true escape literature and in them one can run away to a genuine but different world where virtue triumphs and struggle reaps its rewards."[6]

McGinley's definition of this "genuine but different world" is given in her 1940 poem "Address to the Younger Generation," in which she distinguishes between *truth* and *fact* (The epigram for the poem, a quotation from the *American Library Survey Report*, asserts that "Children want facts, not fiction, in their reading."):

> And is it truth you want, and doings factual?
>   Then from the shelves take down these volumes first.
> Here are your heroes. These are real and actual.
>   These will assuage your thirst.
> . . . .
> Your minds are tough, my loves, and with compliance
>   Can bear the truth. So see you get it learned,
> How there are ghosts and dragons, yes, and giants,
>   And frogs to princes turned.
> . . . .
> These are the verities, and you are able
>   To comprehend them. Leave your elders with
> Their ever-changing scientific fable,
>   Their blind, Utopian myth.
>
> Leave them their legends built on creeds and isms,
>   Allow them their political fairy tales
> Spun out of conquests, wars and cataclysms,
>   And not-too-holy Grails.
>
> While you, enlightened tots, shall sip the chalice
>   Of perfect knowledge as your peers demand,
> And keep thereby the sanity of Alice
>   Roaming in Wonderland.[7]

These are some of McGinley's beliefs on writing for children. In the 1940's, the first three of her own books for children were published—*The Horse Who Lived Upstairs* (1944), *The Plain Princess* (1945), and *All Around the Town* (1948)—all with illustrations by Helen Stone. Each book is a different type: *The Horse* seems to be a "true" story; *Plain Princess*, a moralistic fairy tale; *Town*, a rhyming alphabet-picture book. Different as they are, however, the three books share one quality: they are well written; and, whether in prose or poetry, they are most obviously not "written down" for their readers.

The Horse Who Lived Upstairs is the story of Joey, the cart horse who lives in a New York apartment building. Discontented with his city life and with pulling Mr. Polaski's vegetable wagon, Joey longs to go to a farm. When he does, however, he finds that there is nothing but hard work, unrelieved by the many pleasantries of his city routine—a pat on his nose here, a carrot there, a sugar lump at another spot. The theme of the story— that Joey is happiest where people love him, no matter how unconventional his life is—is easy (and important) for children to comprehend. The story line is simple; the situation—emphasized by the title—intrigues both boys and girls. McGinley is on familiar ground here, too, as she writes of her beloved New York, and of characters—Joey, Mr. Polaski, the Percheron horse "next door" —who have appeal, who are "likeable."

The book, written in a good prose style, has a variety in the length and tempo of sentences; and it has interest in the moderately simple vocabulary. A key word in the book is *discontented*. Used five times during the story, it appears once as *contented*. The story opens with it: "There was once a horse named Joey who was discontented." It also closes with it: "And he was never discontented again." Because the word is used prominently, readers learn it before the story is over. The word choice, however, did provoke an argument with one editor, Miss McGinley remembers, "I was told to use the word *unhappy,* that youngsters wouldn't understand what *discontented* meant. I held out for the longer, more explicit word and . . . I never got a complaint from parent, librarian or even a young reader." Vocabulary is a means to growth, McGinley believes: "Children must grow as they read, both morally and intellectually. Books should offer them the means to grow—new ideas, new characters, new words, not the same old baby-talk and one- or two-syllable words."[8]

The arrangement of the text by page is also effective. For example, after an introductory section, the first full story page contains three relatively long sentences as McGinley describes Joey's life in his upstairs stall. The three sentences are also varied grammatically: the first includes a series of activities, the second is compound, the third contains a compound object: "So every night when Joey came home, he stepped out from the shafts of the wagon, and into an elevator, and up he went to his stall on the fourth floor of the big brick building. It was a fine stall and Joey was very comfortable there. He had plenty of oats to eat and plenty of fresh straw to lie on."[9] The next page contains just one short sentence, with an appropriate picture: "He even had a window to look out of." The following page restates, with

another single, short sentence: "But still Joey was discontented."
Then the text picks up tempo again. And so, with variety, to
the end.

McGinley's second children's book, *The Plain Princess*, is an
admitted fairy tale—at least it has the trappings of a fairy tale.
Esmerelda was the "plain" princess because she was selfish
and vain. The sought-after prince, Charles Michael, ignored her.
Even her parents admitted she—or they—needed help. So, like
all good fairy-tale occupants, they advertised for that help,
expecting a bit of magic or a quick-working spell. Instead, a
lovely gentlewoman of the village asked that Esmerelda come
to live with her and her five daughters for one year. Dame
Goodwit did not suggest magic; she did not use magic; she only
placed Esmerelda in the midst of five responsible, happy, and
loving young women. She asked only that Esmerelda become
responsible.

As in most tales, the "charm" worked in three sections:
Esmerelda's nose turned up when she realized that other people
had abilities too; when she began appreciating the people around
her, her mouth grew beautiful with a smile at her pride in
the work of her own hands; and her eyes sparkled when she
truly forgot herself, and gave the littlest sister her locket. The
"magic" had taken a year to work. Esmerelda returned home,
but Dame Goodwit and her daughters were invited to live at
court so that Esmerelda could still visit them. And the story
ends, typically for a fairy tale, but with qualifications by the
author—"And everyone lived happily ever after—or at least as
happily as it is possible in this mortal world."[10]

Except for the word *discontented*, McGinley's vocabulary in
her first book was simple. *The Plain Princess*, however, is written
in a much more difficult vocabularly. Words like *contrived,
chagrin, innumerable, gnarled, weilded, tedious* are used frequently. The castle "boasted velvety lawns"; "a delegation of
bicycle experts was dispatched to fetch her the handsomest
bicycle possible." The quick rhythms of the prose tend to carry
the reader over words he might not know (hopefully, of course,
he learns them). This book, like *The Horse Who Lived Upstairs*,
contains much variation in sentence length and rhythm: long
sentences are accented with shorter, motif-setting ones like "For
Esmerelda was plain" or "The Dame was calm but firm."

Since *Princess* is fantasy, it would most likely have trouble
finding a publisher today, with the recent emphasis on "factual"

stories. As some current children's books prove, however, it is difficult to create good reading when the plot and theme consist almost entirely of Billy's learning to tie his shoes. Despite trends in publishing, Miss McGinley is fond of the fairy-tale form: it has the happy endings and the conventional morality which children love.[11] This particular book has sold more than sixty-thousand copies, and it continues to sell.

In 1948 McGinley published *All Around the Town,* an alphabet-picture book describing New York City (many of the poems are relevant to any city, however). McGinley has something to say, even in an alphabet book. She does not use a two- or three-line poem for each letter; her poems are eight, nine, or ten lines long; and they also include as many words as practicable that begin with the chosen letter. For example, we cite this poem on the letter W:

> W's for windows.
> Watch them welcome in the night.
> How they twinkle, twinkle, twinkle
> With the waning of the light!
> There's nothing half so wonderful
> In all the wond'rous town
> As a million winking Windows
> When the dusk is coming down.[12]

Windows, watch, welcome, waning, wonderful, wond'rous, winking—all are pleasantly "charged" as well as beginning with the proper letter. As McGinley depicts the city, it is exciting. The rhythm of the highly accented lines conveys her anticipation to the reader: McGinley's verses are happy ones.

Some of her rhymes are definitely forced (of the bus, she writes that it "bears a shopper store-ward" and "seats are better forward"; "In a taxi to and hence" rhymes with "terrible expense"). A surprising amount of her phrasing is good, however: "J's the jumping Jay-walker,/ A sort of human jeep/ . . . . He turns your knees to jelly/ And the traffic into jam." Here McGinley is able to stay within her word emphasis of J. She leaves that pattern if it is not appropriate, as in this poem written for O, the Organ-grinder.

> O's the Organ-grinder.
> When he opens up with tune
> You're sure that winter's over
> And that kites are coming soon.
> So fetch your hoops and roller-skates

> And wear an April mind.
> If the grinder grinds his organ
> Can the spring be far behind?

Organ, opens, over—and then the rest of the stanza is what suits the mood of the organ-grinder and his melodies. I think there is an occasional lapse into a too-adult viewpoint, as with the *N*-for-neighbors and the *T*-for-taxi poems; but, on the whole, McGinley has managed to write poems that are interesting, fairly accurate, and far above the rhymes this kind of book usually falls prey to.

In 1948, McGinley also published *A Name for Kitty*, her first book for toddlers, in the Simon and Schuster Little Golden Book series. While restricted to very simple plot and language, the book has some good imaginative touches—Grandfather's wearing his red thinking cap as he suggests that the kitty be named "Shoe Leather" (since she would be under foot most of the time). It also had a strong yet easy rhythm:

> So he went to the chickens to try his luck,
>   but the chicks said "Peep" and the hens
>   said "Cluck."
> And "Quack" said the duck when he
>   asked the duck. . . .

It is no accident, as we have indicated, that each of McGinley's children's books is "moral." She has frequently stated that she believes the effects of literature throughout history are immense, and that books can exert a harmful influence as well as a beneficial one. She has been specially concerned with the effect of much modern literature (the "flood of sickness") on young readers.[13]

Feeling as she so vehemently does, McGinley has no recourse but to write cheerful stories, stories which show life as being at least as good as it can be "in this mortal world." It seems reasonable to me, also, that the same discretion—the same optimism, perhaps—that kept McGinley from hate-mongering in her World War II poems, kept her stressing the fair, the happy, the good, in these early books for children. Miss McGinley would not rob modern children of "the sanity of Alice."

CHAPTER *5*

"The Pear on My Plate"

I *Technical Innovation*

M ISS McGinley's poems from the 1950's show several kinds of technical development. There is a steady improvement in the poet's handling of the traditional forms, and, more noticeably, perhaps, there is increasing use of "free" forms. The greatest single change in prosody is, however, McGinley's move from accentual to syllabic verse. In poems like "Portrait of Girl with Comic Book" and "Fourteenth Birthday," the length of each line depends not upon a prescribed number of accented syllables but upon the total syllables—accented and unaccented:

> The Enemy, who wears
> Her mother's usual face
> And confidential tone,
> Has access; doubtless stares
> Into her writing case
> And listens on the phone.
>
> Her fortress crumbles. Spies
> Who call themselves her betters
> Harry her night and day.
> Herself's the single prize.
> Likely they read her letters
> And bear the tale away,
>
> (51)

These stanzas from "Fourteenth Birthday" show the poet's use of a six-syllable line in an *abc, abc* rhyme pattern. The use of rhyme is not necessary to syllabic verse as it is practiced, for example, by Marianne Moore; but McGinley seems to use rhyme even when she departs from the other conventions of traditional form.

"Portrait of Girl with Comic Book" achieves a natural, some- what contemplative tone in its syllabic form:

> Thirteen's no age at all. Thirteen is nothing.
> It is not wit, or powder on the face,
> Or Wednesday matineés, or misses' clothing,
> Or intellect, or grace.

Syllabic form allows the poet a means of reaching a poignant shorter line—a slowing of momentum, a pause midway through each stanza and at the close of each. Bringing three lines of ten or eleven syllables down to a much slower six-syllable line creates a very appropriate movement for this reflective poem. "Or intellect, or grace"—a mother's sympathetic admission quite different in tone from the concerns of the earlier lines—matineés, powder, even wit.

McGinley's skill is even more evident in the second and third stanzas. In the first stanza, the slow fourth line has been used for more serious elements; in the second, the midpoint line also has this function: "Wants nothing, everything." But the fourth line of the second stanza reverses the pattern:

> Has secrets from itself, friends it despises;
> Admits none to the terrors that it feels;
> Owns half a hundred masks but no disguises;
> And walks upon its heels.

Stanza three has no shorter midpoint line, through the fourth line—despite its ten syllables—is certainly a stop in the reader's progression: "Is the one age defeats the metaphor." The seven longer lines of stanza three lead with even greater impact, then, into the closing—the poet's admission that thirteen, once passed, can't really be "quite recalled"—"Not even with pity." The reader sees, finally, how appropriate the form has been for the poet's hesitant nostalgia—she does not know, she cannot define, despite her pity.

McGinley appears to use syllabic verse when her subject matter is more "serious," more personally moving, as in these poems ostensibly about her daughters or in "The Doll House," "Journey Toward Evening," and "Midcentury Love Letter." "Journey" follows the pattern of "Portrait"; it has three lines of from nine to thirteen syllables followed by a shorter line of six:

> Fifty, not having expected to arrive here,
> Makes a bad traveler; grows dull, complains,
> Suspects the local wine, dislikes the service,
> Is petulant on trains,
> And thinks the climate overestimated.

> Fifty is homesick, plagued by memories
> Of more luxurious inns and expeditions,
> Calls all lakes cold, all seas
> Too tide-beset (for Fifty is no swimmer),
> Nor, moving inland, likes the country more,
> Believes the hills are full of snakes and brigands.
> The scenery is a bore,
> Like the plump, camera-hung, and garrulous trippers
> Whose company henceforward he must keep.
> Fifty writes letters, dines, yawns, goes up early
> But not to sleep. He finds it hard to sleep.
>
> (16)

This poem is written in a single stanza. By not dividing the poem into quatrains or some other regular verse pattern, McGinley emphasizes the importance of the sentence. The first sentence here is five lines long; the second, six. Moving with varying rhythm because of different line lengths, both sentences tend to approximate the fluctuations of speech. The shorter sentences toward the end suggest the abruptness of the traveler's actions: he is bored, he dines, he goes to his room, "but not to sleep. He finds it hard to sleep."

"Midcentury Love Letter" follows the stanza division and rhyme pattern of a Shakespearean sonnet. Its rhythm, however, is that of syllabic verse alternating between ten- and eleven-syllable lines. Again, the wide range in the duration of sentences is most effective. The poem begins:

> Stay near me. Speak my name. Oh, do not wander
> By a thought's span, heart's impulse, from the light
> We kindle here.

The octave rises through the next long sentence—

> You are my sole defender
> (As I am yours) in this precipitous night,
> Which over earth, till common landmarks alter,
> Is falling, without stars, and bitter cold.

—and then returns to the slower rhythms of the opening short units: "We two have but our burning selves for shelter./ Huddle against me. Give me your hand to hold" (17). The sestet repeats the pattern of the long sentence—pauses indicated by commas—followed and intensified by the shorter, more emphatic sentences. In this poem, as in many of McGinley's later writings, the important unit of rhythm appears to be the sentence rather than the line.

Miss McGinley considers this particular poem in her 1965 discussion of light and serious poetry. She sees the main differences between light and serious verse as being "impact"—and the means by which that impact is achieved. "Serious poetry engages the emotions. Light verse aims at the intellect which it wishes to amuse and divert. . . . Light verse demands brilliance of execution. The surface must be as glittering as the content; in some cases it *is* the content. . . . But poetry when it is noble enough in aspiration needs few tricks. Too much rhyme, alliteration, nimble meter, may interfere with the thrust of thought."[1] "Mid-century Love Letter," McGinley says, is "serious." "Because the total effect of such a poem ought to be emotion, I used few wiles of language. The rhymes (*light/night* et cetera) are ordinary ones and sometimes not even rhymes but assonance (*wander/defender*). The only hostage I gave to artifice beyond the strict fourteen lines of the sonnet form itself, was the arrangement of alternating feminine and masculine rhymes throughout."[2]

Perhaps "In Praise of Diversity," one of McGinley's best-known poems, can be considered as both serious and light poetry. Written in 1954 as the Columbia University Phi Beta Kappa poem, it was to be (in McGinley's words) "something dignified enough and appropriate enough to be read to the scholarly young. I wanted it to be serious in matter although not sober in tone, topical but not ephemeral, witty without being hilarious."[3] The poem seems to fill all McGinley's anticipations; for, written during the McCarthy era of Senate investigations, the poem stressed the need for differences, for diversity, without making any reference to politics per se. The opening stanza does contain the word *subversive;* undoubtedly, the 1954 audience would associate that adjective, despite its use, with the then current situation:

> Since this ingenious earth began
> To shape itself from fire and rubble;
> Since God invented man, and man
> At once fell to, inventing trouble,
> One virtue, one subversive grace
> Has chiefly vexed the human race.
>
> (291)

The first eight stanzas develop the theme that "Difference is the mortal law" but that man doesn't recognize that principle: " 'For or Against' is the only rule." "One shrill, monotonous, level note/ The human orchestra's reduced to." Stanza nine opens with an alternation in content, "Or so it seems. Yet who would dare/ Deny that nature planned it other,/ When every freckled thrush can wear/ A dapple various from his brother. . . ." After a succession of illustrations of diversity ("Twelve months, nine muses, and two sexes"), McGinley closes her poem with the idea of the Trinity:

> Praise what conforms and what is odd,
> Remembering, if the weather worsens
> Along the way, that even God
> Is said to be three separate Persons.
> Then upright or upon the knee,
> Praise Him that by His courtesy,
> For all our prejudice and pains,
> Diverse His Creature still remains.[4]

One of the most interesting things about this poem is its form, or, rather, the comments Miss McGinley makes about its rhythm and rhyme structure: "Since the poem would be heard rather than seen, I decided on utilizing the accent of conservation. That meant the lines must walk, not dance. For my purposes a quatrain followed by a couplet seemed apt. But the meter should run to four and not five stresses, thus ensuring a certain vivacity lacking in iambic pentameter."[5] The shape and pace must suit, therefore, the needs of the poem and, at times, the occasion for the poem. That Miss McGinley felt "In Praise of Diversity" succeeded is evident since she also chose this poem to read at the White House Arts Festival in 1965, and since she placed it as an Envoy to *Times Three*.

The ability to suit technique and tone to each poem as a total impression is nowhere more evident than in McGinley's writing of the 1950's. In addition to the newer practices already mentioned, McGinley works well in a kind of inverted blank-verse pattern—end rhyme is a constant while line length alternates between long (ten to twelve syllables) and short (five or six):

> Our cook is in love. Love hangs on the house like a mist.
> It embraces us all.
> The spoons go uncounted. Confused is the grocery list,
> But light each footfall.
>
> (88)

The very disproportion of these opening lines from "Eros in the Kitchen" creates much of McGinley's intended humor. An even more intricate rhyme pattern adds a kind of suppressed glee to her tirade "Against Hope." "A Certain Age," too, shows her command of exacting stanza forms—here, seven-line stanzas rhyming *aabcdcd*—which are molded to the needs of the poem being written.

In this age of experimentation for the sake (sometimes) of experimentation, McGinley delights in using the most difficult of the traditional forms with her usual expert hand. The poem she selected to include in *Poet's Choice* is "Ballade of Lost Objects," a "piece of pyrotechnics." Of her use of the rigid French form, McGinley says, "I love verse skills and feel I have demonstrated here that ornamental forms can carry a certain weight of thought and poignancy."[6]

> Where are the ribbons I tie my hair with?
>   Where is my lipstick? Where are my hose—
> The sheer ones hoarded these weeks to wear with
>   Frocks the closets do not disclose?
> Perfumes, petticoats, sports chapeaux,
>   The blouse Parisian, the earring Spanish—
> Everything suddenly ups and goes.
>   *And where in the world did the children vanish?*
>
> This is the house I used to share with
>   Girls in pinafores, shier than does.
> I can recall how they climbed my stair with
>   Gales of giggles, on their tiptoes.
> Last seen wearing both braids and bows
>   (But looking rather Raggedy-Annish),
> When they departed nobody knows—
>   Where in the world did the children vanish? . . .
>   (52)

McGinley considers this poem light verse ("The shape makes it so") even though its final effect may be "serious or at least wistful." The ballade form demands the three eight-line stanzas with the four-line envoi; the intricate rhyme pattern of six *A*'s, eight *C*'s, and fourteen *B*'s. "The technique lies," McGinley explains, "in making the rhymes fall naturally on the ear and of changing the refrain's connotation each time it occurs."[7]

Like the highly polished "My Six Toothbrushes," "Ballade of Lost Objects" shows McGinley's tireless poetic skills. Unlike the toothbrush poem, however, the ballade relates thematically to many of McGinley's best poems of the 1950's. "If I have done anything original," McGinley writes in 1965, "it is in my portrayals of childhood and adolescence, not subjects generally attempted—or bothered with."[8] The progression of thought pleases McGinley in this poem since most ballades are only catalogues. And, as she restated the theme of "Ballade" in her comments for *Poet's Choice,* "The human pathos of having one's children grown up and past their homes is as full of truth as, say, a tragic love affair—and much more frequent."[9] McGinley's best poems of this decade show again and again those moments of truth in the life of any woman and/or person. Her best poetry has moved from timely concerns to timeless ones.

One of the most interesting of poems about an adolescent is the lightly phrased "Homework for Annabelle." The mother's hopeless sympathy for her daughter does not darken the tone nor the shape of the poem, which moves in iambic tetrameter and trimeter. Using homework as the objective focus, McGinley drives home her ironic ignorance by means of a refrain:

> A = bh over 2.
>   3.14 is π.
> But I'd forgotten, if I ever knew,
>   What R's divided by.
> Though I knew once, I'd forgotten clean
> What a girl must study to reach fifteen—
> How V is Volume and M's for Mass,
> And the hearts of the young are brittle as glass.
>   (50)

If I ever knew sets the atmosphere of doubt. Although the mother's state is championed a little by "Though I knew once," the second stanza opens with "I had forgotten," and her complacency is double damned with the phrase, "and half with pride." The picture of the mother as she sits "at Annabelle's side/ Learning my lessons over" is too vividly established to be lightened by the remaining quick rhythms and the many references to homework. "And heart is a burden that has to be borne"—for mothers as well as for their children.

In this poem as in much of her writing about "childhood and adolescence," McGinley is skirting dangerous ground. Because she is a woman and a mother, she is open immediately to the charge of "sentimentality." She herself has answered this objection by quoting G. K. Chesterton, "the meanest fear is the fear of sentimentality"; for writing must contain "genuine emotion" if it is to be effectual.[10] At least partly, McGinley's technical prowess here (such a touch as the alternating rhyme pattern in the quatrains of each stanza) keeps this poem—and many others—from any such criticism of sentimentality.

McGinley's choices of subject matter in these poems—and the attitudes she expresses toward them—are well summarized in her short poem, "Apologia":

> When I and the world
> Were greener and fitter,
> Many a bitter
> Stone I hurled.
> Many a curse
> I used to pitch
> At the universe,
> Being so rich
> I had goods to spare;
> Could afford to notice
> The blight on the lotus,
> The worm in the pear.
> But needier grown
> (If little wiser)
> Now, like a miser,
> All that I own
> I celebrate
> Shamefacedly—
> The pear on my plate,
> The fruit on my tree,
> Though sour and small;
> Give, willy-nilly,
> Thanks for the lily,
> Spot and all.

(101)

"All that I own/ I celebrate"—family, home, village. McGinley "owns" the things she loves by assuming a responsibility for them, by caring for them. And the quick tenderness which her writing of the 1950's evinces has become as much a part of the present McGinley attitude as her perceptive view and her wry humor.

II Children's Books, 1950's

McGinley's children's books in this decade are logical outgrowths of her interests in the previous period. *The Horse Who Had His Picture in the Paper* is, in fact, a second story of Joey; he still lives "upstairs," but this time he has an antagonist other than his own desires. The *B* for *bus* from *All Around the Town*

has its own book, *Blunderbus,* this time in prose. There are no
fairy tales per se, but the qualities that made *The Plain Princess*
good reading reappear in *The Most Wonderful Doll in the
World, Lucy McLockett,* and *The Year Without a Santa Claus.*
The fairy-tale elements in *The Make-Believe Twins* are expressed
as the children's pretended adventures. Like her poetry in the
1950's, McGinley's books for children show increasing technical
innovation. More are in poetry—or a mixture of poetry and prose.
The stories of *The Make-Believe Twins,* though written in poetry,
are printed as prose paragraphs in the book.

McGinley's prose account of Blunderbus, "the bus with a mind
of his own,"[11] is especially good because of its rhythmically
phrased description. This sympathetic account of the old double-
decker bus, one about to be scrapped even though he loves his
life, includes several adventures which show Blunderbus's "morality"—courtesy, kindness, love of his world and its people. Her
style makes the story palatable as well as readable:

what passengers had liked most about Number Three was his being
a double-decker; and not the sort of double-decker that buses have
turned into nowadays, closed about with glass and sometimes smelling
of stale air and tobacco smoke. Not at all. *His* upper deck was gloriously open to the sun and the wind—and the rain, too, if one minded
about that.

Oh, it had been a fine thing to board Number Three in the old
days, to climb that little back stairway to the top and let yourself
be carried swiftly up the Avenue. It was better than swinging, it
was better than sailing. . . .

Carefully built paragraphs, each with its own rising rhythm;
emphasis through short sentences; and the poet's use of recurring
thematic phrases, here "it was better than swinging, it was better
than sailing"—these devices characterize McGinley's prose. The
use of the word *gloriously* recalls McGinley's attitude about
discontented in *The Horse Who Lived Upstairs* a decade before.
And how apt is the choice of *gloriously*—in both sound and
rhythm—the poet knows full well.

McGinley's love of words and of word play in gay subjects
reaches a peak, I think, in her 1957 *The Year Without a Santa
Claus*:

> Curious
> Furious
> Fidgety year
> When Santa Claus

> Unhitched his sleigh
> And vowed he was taking a holiday.[12]

The subject of the tale—Santa's "vacation" and the disappointed
but sympathetic children's reaction (they will send Santa presents
instead)—gives McGinley ample reason to catalogue gifts,
vehicles, and emotions. A "plot", one which might seem a little
thin for a book this long, is most effective because of the brightly
unexpected words she chooses. The "shape" of the long, thin
verses, too, fits the listing framework of the story; and varying
line lengths help intensify rhyme patterns. We should notice in
this representative section how the effects of end rhyme change
with the line length:

> "I will," he cried with his eyes ablaze,
> "Everyone else gets holidays:
> "Sailors and
> Tailors and
> Cooks do,
> Policemen
> And writers of books do;
> Tamers of lions and leopards,
> Preachers and
> Teachers and
> Shepherds;
> Watchmen,
> Scotchmen,
> Spaniards,
> Turks;
> Butchers and bakers and grocery clerks—
> They take time off as Christmas nears.
> All except me.
> So it appears
> That, saint or not,
> It's time I got
> My first vacation in a thousand years."

Following this jaunty declaration, McGinley adds two lines of
slower, more nostalgic description that is suitable since the book
contains the underlying pathos of disappointment—for elves and
deer (and Santa) as well as for the expectant children:

> Out in the stable, nuzzling hay,
> The reindeer dreamed of Christmas Day.

She uses this device again in a longer passage midway through
the book, just before Santa begins to change his mind; and she

attains good contrast with the jogging accents of the major part of the verse.

The Year Without a Santa Claus has become one of Miss McGinley's most popular books. Aside from subject, we can understand why. Kurt Werth's illustrations are wonderfully gay (and representational—McGinley believes children want to recognize what they see[13]). I think, however, that the joy of the story rests, even for children (or, probably, especially for children), in the words: the unexpected choice in sequences like this, for example (italics mine),

> He looked to the left,
> He *stared* to the right.
> He didn't trust his own eye-sight,
> So many, so *merry*,
> So *more* and *more*
> Packages were rolling to his front door.
>
> Smack at his doorsill they thundered,
> A million!
> A thousand!
> A hund'erd!

Or this passage, where the sequence of adverbs adds to the affirmation of the story:

> For yearly, *newly,*
> Faithfully, *truly,*
> Somehow
> Santa Claus
> ALWAYS COMES.

Lucy McLockett is written in the same verse technique (catalogues, arranged in generally narrow stanzas, with rhyme at intervals instead of in every-other-line locations). McGinley makes an interesting addition with prose sections (printed in green rather than black) which counterpoint the intent of the poetry. The abrupt change in pace of the prose statements adds gentle humor to Lucy's story of how she "couldn't seem to hold on to anything." These few lines describing Lucy before her dilemma set in illustrate McGinley's various line lengths for differing rhyme effects, as well as the contrast provided by the prose:

> At night she hung her clothes on chairs,
> Neatly.

> She always said her prayers,
> Washed back of her ears,
> Scrubbed under her chin,
> And when she was called she came
> *Right in.*

And that isn't easy, you know, when you are playing a very interesting game outside.[14]

When Lucy loses her shoe on the way to school, her troubles begin in earnest:

> The First Grade
> Couldn't help but grin
> When Lucy McLockett
> Came limping in,
> Late and grimy, her hair ribbon gone,
> One shoe off,
> One shoe on.

At recess, her mother had to drive to school and bring her home in the car.

Lucy's troubles end a bit more unrealistically than do Dulcy's in *The Most Wonderful Doll in the World.* Lucy's forgetfulness ends when her new tooth grows in—and when she remembers to think. Dulcy's problems of dissatisfaction and exaggeration end when she can distinguish between the real and the imaginary.

"There was once a little girl named Dulcy who found it hard to be satisfied with things as they are,"[15] the story opens. When Dulcy loses her doll Angela, a gift from a neighbor, she is dissatisfied with all other playmates. Written in prose, the book is full of conversation between Dulcy and other people; and in Dulcy's descriptions of Angela, McGinley shows her good understanding of a child's mind. Angela is the most wonderful doll ever, as Dulcy's refrainlike dialogues prove:

"I had a doll named Angela and I lost her. And she was the most wonderful doll in the world. She had real yellow hair and eyes that opened and closed and she could say Mama and Papa and sing Rockaby Baby. And she wore patent leather shoes with heels and she could wave her hand. And take steps. She had a purse with a handkerchief in it and little tiny leather gloves."

"But look—this doll has a skating costume," Aunt Tabby coaxed.

Dulcy stopped and thought about that for a time. "So did Angela," she cried. "And she had skates, too, that you could take off and put on. And when you wound her up, *she skated.*"

When spring comes and Dulcy finds the real Angela again, she realizes the theme of the book: "Everybody has a dream. . . . But as we grow up, we learn to be more satisfied with Things as They Are." Dulcy does not "reform," however—and, for this reason, the story seems believable. It concludes when the child is telling her neighbor about Veronica (another "most wonderful doll . . ."), but Dulcy's telling ends with giggles and her confession. She *knows* that Veronica is imaginary. She will, however, continue to have her dream.

In *The Make-Believe Twins*, the twins also know the difference between real and pretend; it just happens that "the game that they like the most, by far, is pretending they're diff'rent from what they are."[16] The eight adventures of Peter and Penny, the Parker twins, re-create the children's making believe that they are lions, Eskimos, pirates, mer-children—"a wonderful sport is Let's Pretend"; and the reader is inclined to agree.

III   The Province of the Heart

With the publication in 1959 of her selected essays, *The Province of the Heart*, Miss McGinley discovered anew what it was to be a "public voice." She had achieved some popular notice through the years, especially after her essay, "Suburbia, Of Thee I Sing," was published in *Harper's* in 1949; but, by and large, her influence had been confined to readers of her poetry. As she shamefacedly wrote in the introduction to the book, Mc-Ginley had "committed" a book of prose; readers of these essays were not surprised, however. McGinley's prose style had much in common with her poetry—exact yet apparently colloquial; personal, in that the poet was often the speaker of the essay; honest, in that her opinions echoed and reinforced those already expressed in her poems.

The Province of the Heart restates McGinley's premises in her defense of suburbia. But the collection does much more than defend the cosy neighborhood where women might thrive on their homey pastimes; it emphasizes again and again the right of women to do just that—thrive. (D. P. Hobby has called these essays "gentle lectures on the joys of being all the things modern fiction deplores: married, feminine, suburban, maternal, adjusted, middle-aged, and unanalyzed"[17]). But, even in the age of feminine *mystiques*, McGinley has asserted that most women's places are necessary ones—in their homes; and they should be admired, loved, for loving their life's work. Only the "three-handed" woman should attempt an outside career, for being a wife and mother demands the same kinds—and amounts—of energy that a career outside the home does.

Even though McGinley makes unquestionably valid points throughout these essays, critics—when they have objected to *Province*—have done so because of this cautionary tone. "McGinley has done it," they chant. "She's had a career. Who does she think she's kidding?" No one. McGinley as author has described often the frustrations, the difficulties, of being a writer in the midst of being everything else: "I have seen how my male contemporaries work, how their writing hours are guarded, their meals brought into their studies on trays, the house silenced while they create. That sort of Eden I lost along with Eve."[18] Her point is simply that her writing has usually come second—because she has wanted it, willed it, to come second.

The reasons for McGinley's choice are the subjects of her other essays: the complicated but vital relationship between husband and wife, the absorption of parents in their children's lives, the essential kindness of people in a community, the respect for privacy (and the need for human dignity). The further we read, the more often we remember McGinley's opening anecdote, a Mr. Edward's retort to Samuel Johnson: "You are a philosopher, Dr. Johnson. I have tried too in my time to be a philosopher; but, I don't know how, cheerfulness was always breaking in."

McGinley's cheerfulness is in no way a blind optimism. She stays within the subjects she knows so that she can speak with authority: children grow up too fast; we should slow them down, McGinley pleads. We should let our daughters know what sin is; but we should also let them learn why a man deserves the respect his family gives him. Divorce has threatened every marriage—more important, however, is the adhesive that keeps marriages together. Although McGinley somewhat defensively entitles Part I of her book "Unorthodoxies," her ingenuous arguments should convince any reader that her view is a right one.

Much of the effectiveness of McGinley's prose goes back to the undeniable personality of the author. Not only does she draw heavily on her children, her husband, and her community for her illustrations and her "proofs"; she also describes her world as though it were one of fact. There is no apology for her limited perspective: McGinley's acceptance of her position makes the reader accept it also.

Although the reader feels sure of McGinley's convictions in

each essay, the author's tone remains light, direct, easy. McGinley never falls into the machine. Her matter-of-factness shows in her unhurried, anecdotal style—the paragraphs are loosely filled with argument but never loosely written. There are many structures in series, many balanced phrases. Often, the weight of an entire passage rests on distinctions made between the forms of one word, as in the conclusion to "The Honor of Being a Woman":

. . . if we have brought no new graces to our society, if we are losing the old ones, we have no right to our rights.

Perhaps we shall have to start earning them [rights] all over again. Our greatest victories have always been moral ones. Without relinquishing our new learning or our immediate opportunities, we must return to a more native sphere. Let us teach our daughters not self-realization at any cost but the true glory of being a woman—sacrifice, containment, pride, and pleasure in our natural accomplishments. Let us win back honor. The honors will take care of themselves.

(*Province*, 22)

The play between *right* and *rights, honor* and *honors,* is worthy of the poet—and the most common praise given to McGinley's prose style is that it is "poetic." What this term means is, simply, I think, that the prose style shows (1) care in word choice, (2) skill in word patterns, and (3) variation appropriate to the subject (the mood of "I Knew Mrs. Tuttle" is far different from that of "In Defense of Sin"). McGinley's sense of the whole—her timing—never lags. One of these essays, "Against Gardens," is sixteen pages long; others are only six or seven. Each is an autonymous structure. We notice the differences in movement, the variety of effects created by the author in this single page from "Against Gardens."

For we found ourselves, seven months of the year, slaves to our bit of property. Sometimes, if we were working with winter bloom, it was twelve.

As slaves, we were willing enough. Gardening has compensations out of all proportion to its goals. It is creation in the pure sense. That dungareed figure scrabbling in the earth, with dirt under his fingernails and thorn scratches on his arms, is no figure of fun but half a god. The sun beats on him, the rain wets him, arthritis lurks under his kneeling pad, ants run up and down his sleeves. Still, it is the posture and the task he dotes on. To be able to walk about a border after dinner and smell the fragrances of his verbena, to speak a personal word to each painted daisy; to pull up a wild onion or congratulate the tuberous begonia he has steered past the nursery stage and into preposterous flower—those are pleasures past explaining. But pleasure can turn into dissipation, as we found to our expense. The beginning, of course, was all hopeful delight. We were early in the trend to the suburbs, early in the now common pattern of a young couple without much money saved, who buy a house in an upper-middle-class area and yearn to make the earth blossom like a Jackson and Perkins Hybrid Perpetual Climbing Rose.

The house *we* bought was an elderly one, and it already had a garden of sorts, running chiefly to cedar planting and effete narcissi. "So much green," we said, pouting. "No color, no plan. What lack of imagination!"

Our own imaginations were vivid enough for three families . . .

(*Province,* 89)

The contrast in the first short paragraph is emphasized through the position of *seven months* early in the sentence, and no less emphasized—rhythmically—in the second echoing sentence with the word *twelve* coming at the end.

Opening the next section, the phrase *as slaves* (a repetition of the "we found ourselves slaves" a few lines before) tells the reader that the short transitional paragraph is about to be developed. The three short, opening sentences, each one covering much information, help set the matter-of-fact tone. McGinley is walking the tight rope between the praise for gardening that she must honestly give ("creation in the pure sense") and the restraint she must achieve. The short sentences imply this control over her praise and her self. The rest of the sentences in the paragraph alternate between long series structures, generally descriptive, and the shorter cryptic "restraint": "But pleasure can turn into dissipation. . . ."

As the long quotation illustrates, McGinley's description works because of her strong adjectives and visual emphasis. The picture of her husband, "dungareed," "scrabbling in the earth," "thorn scratches on his arms," is vivid; but her description of the man's actions is even more emphatic. Uncomfortable, he still "dotes on" not only the task but the posture. His creations are his friends, McGinley tells us later; he will "speak a personal word to each painted daisy" or "congratulate the tuberous begonia." "Preposterous flower," "hopeful delight," "pleasures past explaining"—McGinley's couplings of adjective and noun help create the tone of intentional and humorous exaggeration. "Our own imaginations were vivid enough for three families" is another hyperbole intended for humor.

Structurally, the shorter paragraphs work somewhat as a unit.

The short opening statement about "the beginning" is expanded in the description to follow. As the description progresses, Mc-Ginley uses word repetition as subtle transition: the phrase "early in the" helps establish the similarity of the ideas so coupled. "Buy a house" appears in the next sentence (the flow of meaning continues despite the new paragraph) as "The house *we* bought." The pouting comments of the young homeowners—and Mc-Ginley's use of direct quotation is as characteristic in her writing as it is wise—"What lack of imagination!" leads to the opening sentence of the following paragraph, "Our own imaginations. . . ."

There are many thematic ties between McGinley's prose and poetry. Her concern for the happiness of children comes through in several strong poems, but a different view of the problem absorbs her interest in her essays. Taking as a whole her writing on the subject of children, we find a consistent opinion. It is as if the poet needed another medium to finish her "presentation": the material the essays include is nearly always different from that of the poems. Despite the similarity in theme between some poems and corresponding essays, there is very little actual "overlapping." The opening of the 1944 essay, "I Knew Mrs. Tuttle," is an exception because it does remind one of McGinley's earlier poem in the 1934 *On the Contrary*, "Complaint." In this case of comparison between forms, the essay seems to be a stronger presentation of the subject, which is the author's failure to meet "characters." McGinley did not include the poem in her 1960 selected poems, *Times Three;* the essay does reappear in *Province*. Each version opens with the mention of the author's "lack":

> There seems some fatal lack in me,
> A curious infirmity
> By fault whereof I never can
> Discern the picturesque in Man.[19]

And in the essay, "It must be that I lack a certain inner warmth possessed and exploited by my more spectacular friends."

In the essay form, "possessed and exploited" is a quick fore-shadowing of the point McGinley makes her poem's conclusion: "other folk are always lighting on/ (And getting quite well paid for writing on.)." The essay progresses instead to the "consolation," the fact that the poet had known Mrs. Tuttle. Mrs. Tuttle *is* the essay. The three-paragraph introduction of the essay covers the same subjects as the twenty-two-line poem—the author's

lament followed by a list of some noteworthy people: "A taxi
driver who reads Proust" is shaped in "Complaint" as

> No taxi driver, caught or cruising,
> Has ever uttered an amusing
> Oath, mot, reproof, or epigram
> In my vicinity.

The couplet rhyme pattern in the poem is too restrictive, I think,
for enough meaningful details to be used. Later in the poem,
several sentences are inverted, again to enable the poet to meet
the demands of the rhyme pattern.

Another passage of the poem describes a waiter:

> And if, forgetting his high station,
> A waiter grants me conversation,
> I find his comments rather leaning
> To entrees than Life's Inner Meaning.

—but the prose waiter is much more real: "The shabby waiter
who fetches my filet of sole may wear the lines of suffering in his
patient face, but whether from nostalgia or bunions I will never
learn. The utmost information I can pry out of him concerns
the fact that there's no more spumoni today and he doesn't know
about the apple cake" (*Province*, 114). The author can maintain
her ironic tone ("utmost information," "lines of suffering") and
bring it down nicely ("bunions," "no more spumoni today," "he
doesn't know about the apple cake"), free as she is from a prescribed rhythm and rhyme pattern.

Some of the same comparisons might be made between Mc-
Ginley's essays on suburbia and her poems on that subject.
Bette Richart, for one, thinks most of McGinley's poems about
suburbia are bad—too coy, too complacent[20]—and, we might add,
too vague. The piles of well-described details McGinley can
include in the easy rhythms of her prose reinforce her views just
as they help build the tone that is so important to this kind of
exposition. But most of McGinley's poems about the suburbs
are written (during the 1940's) in highly restrictive forms—
"Sonnets from the Suburbs"—and some of the details that are
included seem chosen for "fit" rather than for relevance. Too
many of these poems are ostensibly "light verse." "The 5:32" is
one of the best, but many of the others ("Beauty Parlor,"
"Suburban Newspaper") are so slight in subject that their
formal shape seems incongruous. A more serious objection might
be that such poems as "P.T.A. Tea Party," "Occupation: House-

wife," and "Country Club Sunday" profess attitudes that Mc-
Ginley the essayist abandons in prose—for she has, as a poet, at
times been guilty of championing the "wrong" views of suburbia.

Almost without exception, McGinley's essays are written after
the poems which relate to the same subject. We must allow,
therefore, for some change in the author's view. But more and
more frequently, McGinley seemingly turns to prose as a chance
to get it all said. The chance to write for magazines is not unwelcome, she confesses.[21] It is not unwelcome, we might suppose,
this chance to say it all. But, in retrospect, the reader who knows
McGinley's poetry cannot help but remember that early poem,
"Ballad of the Lord and Columbus." It could well be that the
love expressed in *The Province of the Heart* essays began with
her defense of "Christopher Columbus, sturdy old tar," as he
praised crowded, raucous America:

> "A proud young race and their children and their sires,
> Dwelling in their houses, working at their fires;
> And some were weeping,
>   And some were old,
> And some were sleeping,
>   Hungry and cold,
> And some here wailing for the times askew,
> But, Lord, it was better than the world I knew.
>
> "Tanned and tall were their sons and their daughters.
> They had won the valleys, they had tamed the waters.
> I saw them soaring
>   Through the conquered air.
> Their trains went roaring
>   Everywhere.
> Strong their buildings and their bridges stood.
> The land was fertile and the harvests good.
> And a hundred million people
>   Lived in brotherhood. . . .
>   (287-88)

CHAPTER 6

Unapologies

I *Poetry in the 1960's*

PHYLLIS McGinley's career as a poet reached a kind of apex in 1960 with the publication of *Times Three: Selected Verse from Three Decades,* for the book won the 1961 Pulitzer Prize for Poetry. It also won for McGinley an even wider recognition, for the book was consistently good: its contents had been well "selected" for balance, variety in technique, and subject. Besides omitting poems dated by their references (to Petrillo, the Dionne quintuplets, movie stars, comic strips), McGinley left out many good poems which are technically similar; for fifteen early "timely" poems written in the same general form are less representative of the whole course of McGinley's poetry than single poems from the same period which show more innovation in shape. Readers may miss favorite poems, but the three hundred published give the best possible overview of McGinley's poetry. Seventy new poems appear in the 1950's section; and among them are many of the poet's strongest (see chapters 1 and 5).

McGinley's evident facility with various forms in these poems from the 1950's is a tribute to the poetic discipline she has always believed in—and practiced: "Discipline is the groundwork of all art. The abstract painter has to know first how to draw, the symbolist to write ordinary lines. And the poet, no matter how soon he intends to throw overboard his formalism, has first to be capable of a correctly rhymed and metered stanza."[1]

As McGinley's worksheets for her poems show, she makes many changes between the first draft and the final. Line after line, word after word, is moved into different position or disappears, only to reappear in another place. W. H. Auden has defined the poet as one who loves to play with words; and most appropriately, wrote the very complimentary introduction for McGinley's *Times Three.* The essence of creating a poem seems to be to McGinley the crystallization of the poet's long labor with words, and his equally long love of them. As she describes the process of writing:

There is such a thing as inspiration (lower case), but it is no miracle. It is the reward handed to a writer for hard work and good conduct. It is the felicitous word sliding, after hours of evasion, obediently into place. It is a sudden comprehension of how to manufacture an effect, finish off a line or a stanza. At the triumphant moment this gift may seem like magic, but actually it is the result of effort, practice, and the slight temperature a sulky brain is apt to run when it is pushed beyond its usual exertions.[2]

And of the sometimes greater prowess, the greater ease, of the more practiced poet, McGinley writes: "As a basketball player after long practice does not need to measure his shots from the floor but knows by coordination of eye and muscle just how the ball will best enter the basket, so a poet achieves effects sub-consciously—and, again, after long practice."[3] It is the fruit of this long practice, as well as the very interesting course of the practice itself, that *Times Three* so clearly shows.

Critical reception to the volume was enthusiastic. There was less of the belittling tone occasionally taken by those reviewers who prefer "serious" poetry. Many critics—taken off balance by Auden's long paean to McGinley as the most *feminine* of women writers—"forgot" to deplore the fact that she was a woman. The scope and sweep of those three hundred poems were too great for cursory comment. For the first time, a McGinley book received literary commentary rather than critical gossip. David McCord's praise in *Saturday Review* was based on what he saw as McGinley's progress during the three decades: in the 1930's, he considered the poems good despite the overuse of feminine rhyme and too little experimentation; the poems of the 1940's showed a greater interest in innovation and more ability "to sustain a single objective mood." And in the late poems McCord saw less gaiety, sharper satire; and the fact that "form assumes a new importance." Before we could quarrel with his comment about satire, he added that there is much more compassion in these poems, more freedom of a kind he would ascribe to intuition.[4] It seems a fair overview, one which would parallel McGinley's own comment in 1960, "I've been building up, trying to get better. At first, back in the thirties, I was writing real light verse. I mean *really* light verse. . . . But I've been moving toward something a little different—poetry of wit."[5]

The 1960 *Times Three* was McGinley's last book of poetry until 1967 when *A Wreath of Christmas Legends* was published. Although some critics viewed the book of fifteen poems as a seasonal contribution, McGinley readers were enthusiastic about the legends as poetry. In direct line of descent from her series of poems on saints ("Reformers, Saints, and Preachers") and her many poems about Christmas, this collection gave McGinley another chance to write about her often recurring theme: love. Using Jesus's birth as the ostensible center, McGinley focuses on the emotion of love—or the lack of it—in most of these poems.

A Wreath of Christmas Legends made clear, too, that an expert craftsman had succeeded in writing single poems in which rhythm, form, and language expressed perfectly each story being told. The subject matter might sound limiting; but as McGinley handles each legend, we are conscious only of her great ease and her great technical freedom that are displayed in a wide variety of forms.

The slow, heavily alliterative lines of "Legend of the Holly" (published in 1966 as "Ballad of the Holly") are in keeping with the form chosen for the poem as well as the story to be told about how

> the little Newborn
> Has pricked His finger upon a thorn,
> Has left His blood on the spiny leaves.
> Heavy of heart the holly grieves . . .
> (*Wreath*, 61)

The use of *h* not only shows the line; it also emphasizes the necessary capitalization of the sacred pronoun. For in these lines, Christ is the central figure, although earlier—and later—the holly assumes the center of the stage. Lines surrounding this section contain many slow *n, m, s,* and *f* sounds ("nothing of note," "sorrow and shame," "Mary the Mother," "fair and foul"). The forgiving words of Mary stay within this sonority, but they move to a slower, deeper conclusion as the soft *w* sound dominates:

> And you, dear tree, are the innocent
> Who weeps for pity what man might do.
> So all your thorns are forgiven you.

With Mary's forgiveness comes a brighter tempo: the iambic rhythm becomes more insistent—"now red, rejoicing, the berries shine/ On jubilant doors as a Christmas sign."

Most of the lines in the poem are regular iambic tetrameter.

With the slowing of the section in which Mary speaks, rhythm also seems to be more pronounced. Occasionally, the four beats are located within single words, often monosyllabic ones. The intensity of such separation is also a slowing device:

> Heavy of heart the holly grieves,
>
> Sees in a terrible vision how
> A crown of holly shall bind His brow
> When Child is man.
>
> For sorrow and shame
> The berries have blushed as red as flame.
> Says Mary the Mother,
> "Take no blame.

The expert use of pause in, particularly, "When Child is man" and "Take no blame," is also evident in that first line of refrain, "Raise high the holly." This parenthetical refrain which both opens and closes the poem—helping it to stay within the ballade tradition—is not mere repetition. The opening lines are a fairly standard admonition, a general comment:

> The holly berry that burns so red
> (*Raise high the holly!*)
> Once was whiter than wheaten bread.
> (*As love is better than folly.*)

The closing, with only a slight change in wording, manages to relate specifically to the legend just recounted:

> . . . desolation to joy makes way.
> (*Hang high the holly!*)
> Holly is the symbol of Christ's Birthday.
> (*When love shall vanquish folly.*)

Another ballad in this collection makes use of the more typical ballad stanza: the quatrain with alternately rhyming lines. "Ballad of the Nightingale," however, is not written in iambic measure. For the most part, McGinley uses an anapestic line. The liberties she takes with a set pattern are typical of her responsiveness to the needs of each poem. Measure is not rigid anapest; and two of these stanzas have five lines.

The gently pulsing dimeter lines provide a soft rhythmic background for the story of the nightingale that is rewarded by Mary for its love of the Christ Child. McGinley's method of narrating the story, too, is appropriately musical—key phrases are repeated, sometimes relating stanzas.

> Hark! when on hill and dale
> Hang the night-hushes,
> Then sings the nightingale,
> Sole among thrushes.
>
> Sole among thrushes, she
> Pours out of shadow . . .
>   (*Wreath*, 53)

Similarly, the fourth stanza closes "There was a child that lay/
Cold in a manger"; the fifth restates the important adjective,
cold, in the opening phrase, "cold in his narrow bed. . . ."
Repetition, as well as much use of alliteration, within these poems
is characteristic of the ballad form—the literary devices serving
also as mnemonic aids and, as Coleridge saw, as a means of
discharging excessive emotion. Characteristic, too, are the plunge
into the story and the use of dialogue within the poem—in this
case, Mary's speech to the nightingale. Also in the method of the
balladeer is McGinley's use of the mood-setting, initial stanza
which is repeated at the end of the poem with slight but telling
variations: the nightingale becomes "Queen among thrushes"
after Mary's praise. In the early stanza, she was described as
"Sole among thrushes."

Nor can McGinley's choice of words within these ballads—
"Ballad of the Rosemary" and "Ballad of the Robin" included—
be judged independently of poetic conventions. Just as the
balladeer stays within the simple colloquial vocabulary, so does
McGinley employ phrases like "hill and dale," "night-hushes,"
"dark and danger," "the little Newborn," "heavy of heart," and
"Hark!" Word order is sometimes inverted; modifying phrases
precede nouns—syntactically, too, McGinley follows the older
tradition. The result is a poem that maintains the reverent
clarity of the early Christian ballad—but at the same time achieves
an autonomy of its own.

"Why the Owl Wakes at Night" also uses some ballad conventions. Much of the story is told through dialogue. The Wise
Men call to the birds to accompany them; the birds go willingly,
singing, "A kingly Child/ Is waiting for us." Only the owl questions, "Who is He/ That bids me follow?" "Who? Who? . . .
Who, Who?" The sleepy bird does not go to Bethlehem; now,
in mourning, he must ask repeatedly, "Who'll guide me to/ the
small Newborn?/ Who, who? Oh, who?"

The reader notices the phrase "small Newborn" again; the

alliteration of "Fled every fowl/ Forsaking rest" and "Cackling crows"; a few inverted sentences; the traditional simile, "From sleep, like arrows,/ All arose—." Similarity in poetic technique is important in this discussion of McGinley's legend-poems; not so much for itself, but because of the very different poems she has written while employing the same kinds of devices. These recurring forms and language are intended to emphasize the solemn traditions of which—and from which—she writes.

Rhythm in the owl poem is a rough iambic measure, with alternate lines in the quatrain rhyming, very close to the traditional form. Stanzas are regular until the end, when content requires a fifth rhyming line.

> Must for distress
> Stay broad awake
> And comfortless,
> That would not break
> His comfort for Love's sake.
>   (*Wreath*, 37)

The theme of punishment for those who refuse the Christ Child—the owl and Babushka—and reward for those who do special service for Him—the nightingale, rosemary, the robin, the cat—is an important one among these legends, as it is among the many biblical parables. Each small episode of denial, in a sense, symbolizes the Christian admonition, "Whosoever would save his life must lose it." McGinley is no stranger to these precepts, as her earlier writing has shown. Her strength in these poems again lies in her recognition of the total role of any religious belief—that a belief must temper the necessary denial, penitence, and sacrifice with joy in its expression. There can be wit in the midst of fervor, tranquility in the midst of sorrow (see pp. 21-23).

One of the most familiar of the legends, "Story for an Educated Child," shows McGinley's wit to good advantage. In recounting the legend that animals can speak on Christmas Eve, McGinley makes the point that the animals speak in Latin and—as she concludes the poem:

> So many a child might brave the cold
> To hear them talking. But I am told
> *He mustn't be more than six years old.*
> And who at six knows Latin?
>   (*Wreath*, 50)

"Story for an Educated Child" is a clear description of the belief, with excellent sections on the rooster, ox, sheep, and donkey as they converse in Latin. Its close rhyme pattern (*aabccb*) and regular form add to its clarity. McGinley uses an iambic measure, with variation in line lengths helping to moderate the steady pace. Throughout the poem, an iambic tetrameter couplet is followed by a third line of iambic trimeter.

In contrast to the regularity of "Story," we might set "The Legend of the Cat." Again McGinley recounts a belief, this time about the cat who found herself humble and speechless before the Christ. The poem, moving somewhat stealthily itself, is arranged in a kind of quantitative line pattern—some lines have three words; some, eleven. The emphasis placed on each word helps to determine the rate with which the line moves:

> Some winter night
> Observe Cat now. Her eyes will suddenly gleam
> Yellow against the light,
> Her body shudder in a jungle dream . . .
>   (*Wreath,* 40)

The rhyme scheme of this poem is, for McGinley, very irregular. Occasionally, alternate lines rhyme, but there are also couplet rhymes and groups of interlocking five- and six-line rhymes. One reason for McGinley's choice is more use of assonance than usual—deep, full vowel sounds dominate this passage describing the cat's reticence as the other animals praise Jesus:

> Although their anthems lifted all around,
> She, in her throat, made only a trembling sound
> And could not bow her head.
>
> Yet as the morning dawned
> And one by one the other creatures fled
> Each to his habitat—

In its emphasis on sound, "The Legend of the Cat" is certainly in part a tone poem. The key note throughout is the resonant vowel sound, as in the passage just quoted. The poem also opens with it: "At midnight's stroke,/ On the first Christmas, half the world awoke"; and it ends with it: "Then, reassured, she curls herself along/ The floor and hums her cool, domestic song." And the movement of the slow dominant vowels is appropriate as it re-creates the movement of the cat, "shy and wild," which only "approached" the hearth and "lay dumb/ And dazzled there."

Appropriately, McGinley employs some of these same techniques in her songlike poem, "The Canticle of the Bees." Heavy alliteration, musically accented words, the regular trochaic dimeter lines—all reinforce the simple opening description of that "honey-havened people":

> Bees in winter
> Weather keep,
> Rapt, a garden-haunted
> Sleep,
>
> Dream of summer,
> Still as stone,
> Save on Christmas Eve,
> Alone. . . .
>
> (*Wreath*, 21)

In the middle section of this poem—the bees' song proper, as well as in the central section of the "Cat" poem—McGinley uses an arrangement new to her poetry: that of a staggered left margin and an aligned right margin.

> "Praise Him,"
> Sing the choiring bees,
> "Lord of limes
> And locust trees,

Besides emphasizing the rhyme words, this pattern forces the reader to a sharper realization of the lines' differing movements. "The Stork," "The Pine Tree," "The Night," and "The Birthday" are arranged similarly.

Another innovation in typographical layout is the pattern of "The Star's Story," a poem in which McGinley uses the rhyme scheme she had come to admire in the earlier "Lesson for Beginners," *abcd, abcd*:

> When the great Star shone
> From its mighty station
> So shepherds, tranced,
> Knelt down in the dew,
> It was not alone
> In its jubilation.
> The little stars danced
> By the thousands, too.
>
> (*Wreath*, 25)

Just as the rhyme progresses down the stanza of the poem, so does the indentation of successive lines—raylike, we assume.

Such noticeable innovation in form, rhyme, and measure is more striking when we consider the earlier poems McGinley had written about these Christmas legends. To my knowledge, three earlier poems were published: "How the Beasts Keep Christmas" and "The Ballad of Befana" in the 1957 *Merry Christmas, Happy New Year* (a collection that included poems from the 1930's and 1940's), and "A Christmas Legend" published in *McCall's* in 1959. None of these poems is included in the 1967 *Legends*. Though each poem describes a different legend, all are written in relatively strict iambic measure and are arranged, for the most part, in quatrains. McGinley's omission of these early poems—and her recasting of several of them, or the material from them—suggests her own dissatisfaction with their original forms.

The earlier "How the Beasts Keep Christmas" describes, in short dimeter lines, the various animals' reverence:

> At midnight's stroke,
> In barn, in stall,
> Kneel all
> The dumb folk.
>
> Meekly bow
> In reverence, then,
> The silly hen,
> The horned cow . . .[6]

The quick movement of the lines, accented through the line-end punctuation, is less appropriate to a mood of reverence than the measures the poet uses in the two poems from *A Wreath of Christmas Legends* which bear some resemblance to this earlier poem. One of them, "The Legend of the Cat," opens with the same phrase, but the second much longer line slows the momentum effectively:

> At midnight's stroke,
> On the first Christmas, half the world awoke.
> Then out of nest and lair
> Came thronging to Bethlehem the wordless folk;

The listing of the animals in this poem appears as "things of fur and feather/ (The deer beside the lion, the pheasant, the hare/ Safe in the fox's paws) bent down together." In the earlier poem the fox-and-hare image, which is weaker in language, appears at the end of a rhyme-dominated quatrain:

> And glory wheels
> Through den and lair.
> Beside the hare
> Fox kneels,

Another later poem, "The Stork," also makes use of the reverent animals, "The birds and the beasts knelt down to pray." By alternating stanzas of long lines with short-lined quatrains, McGinley creates a needed variation in tempo.

> In wonder all,
> Adoring, kneeled—
> The ox in his stall,
> The fox in the field,
>
> While badger and bear and each wild thing
> Flocked round the manger where slept a King . . .
> (*Wreath*, 9)

Another very interesting change can be seen in "The Ballad of Befana" which I assume to be the early version of "A Legend from Russia." In the later poem, the Wise Men ask the good housewife Befana to come with them "to greet the Child," and she replies: " 'Oh, happily, happily would I fare,/ Were my dusting through and I'd polished the stair.' "[7] Her work keeps her from the journey, from even sending gifts. When Befana later searches for the Child, she could not find him. "And still she wanders at Christmastide,/ Houseless, whose house was all her pride." Then she spreads her message, "Put off your toiling and let love in."

In the later poem, Babushka, the grandmother, becomes a more sympathetic figure than the good Befana had been. "Grandmother, grandmother, old and wise" becomes the symbol of the world's weariness—and McGinley works with assonance to create a sonorous measure, one intensified by two words central to the theme of the poem, *Grandmother* and *Tomorrow*. We should notice the long, open vowels of the slow (weary) opening:

> Babushka, the Grandmother, snug in her room,
> Sat nodding and nodding over her loom,
>
> Sat suppered and snug with no desire
> But a welcoming bed and an ample fire. . . .
> (*Wreath*, 29)

In this poem, McGinley more plausibly has the shepherds—not the Wise Men—bother Babushka; and she refuses them:

Babushka listened, nodding anew.
"Tomorrow," she murmured. "Tomorrow will do.

"I'll bring the best from my cupboard's store.
Tomorrow."
          The shepherds knocked no more.

The Babushka poem is much longer than "Ballad of Befana,"
partly because of the exigencies of tone, partly because of an
inclusion of relevant detail. In the early version, McGinley says
simply, "Then, gifts in her hands. . . ." But, in "A Legend from
Russia," the gifts are described, lovingly:

> Loaves and oranges, cakes and meat,
>
> A shawl for the Lady, soft as June,
> For the Child in the Crib a silver spoon,
>
> Rattles and toys and an ivory game.

The gifts are emphasized at least partly because they become
the peasant woman's "message": she does not preach homilies to
the people. Instead,

> Babushka creeps
>
> Silently, hopefully, up the stair
> And leaves three gifts from her basket there—
>
> One to marvel at, one to enjoy,
> And one for the Kingly Boy.

The most interesting changes between the early legend poems
and the later ones occur in the progression from the 1959 "A
Christmas Legend," which includes the stores of both the robin
and the nightingale, to the later separate poems, "Ballad of the
Robin" and "Ballad of the Nightingale." McGinley seems to have
realized the true rhythmic and tonal possibilities of each legend
only in the later versions. "A Christmas Legend" tells the same
stories, but it does so much less effectively. Alternating between
the two stories forces the poem into an almost singsong pattern;
first the nightingale, then the robin. Again, variation in tone is
difficult to achieve in these short, regularly accented and rhymed
lines:

> The dark came down, the frost
>   came down,
> And the small fire burnt low.

> Sighed Mary, "Who will kindle
> These embers to a glow?"

> > The Child is stirring from His sleep
> > This midnight of the year.
> > Oh! who will sing a measure
> > For comfort at His ear?[8]

The answers to Mary's questions come in the next alternating stanzas, which are phrased similarly even though the situations differ in intensity: the nightingale stays awake to sing, but the robin's breast is burned in his task of fanning the fire.

In the later poems, McGinley is able to create the very different effects of each bird's acts. Although the ballad structure is the same in each poem, rhythms and line arrangement differ noticeably. "Ballad of the Nightingale" moves quickly in trochaic dimeter lines (see p. 97); "Ballad of the Robin" moves in tetrameter lines of iambic feet accented with dactylic, as may be seen in the following quotations from each poem:

(the nightingale)	(the robin)
Him once she comforted	Bravest of small created things,
With her sweet trilling;	He made a bellows of his wings.
Sad that a babe should lie	He puffed his feathers to a fan,
So undefended,	Singing, until the ash began
Sang Him a lullaby	
Till the night ended,	To kindle, glow, to burn its best.
(*Wreath*, 54)	The flame leaped out. It seared
	his breast,
	(*Wreath*, 46)

In these poems as in the Befana-Babushka legends, the quality of McGinley's language is much stronger in the later poems. "His [the robin's] wings and his feathers/ He plied like a fan" becomes "He made a bellows of his wings,/ He puffed his feathers to a fan." "Till the ashes were kindled/ And the red warmth began" appears in the later poem as "until the ash began/ To kindle, glow, to burn its best." Particularly effective lines like "So all the stable was beguiled/ To warmth. And softly slept the Child." have no antecedent in the early poem.

Phrasing in the 'reward" sections of the three poems again shows varying degrees of language skill. In the earlier "Legend," Mary praises the nightingale with this quatrain,

> Oh, you who coaxed the little Lord
> This night to shut His eyes
> Ecstatically forever
> Shall sing but lullabies.

The somewhat cloying tone of *coaxed, little, lullabies,* and *ecstatically* is changed to the latter majestic praise in "Ballad of the Nightingale."

> You brought your song to Him,
> All the night long to Him,
> You and no other.
>
> Lone on your leafy bough,
> Brave though imperiled,
> You shall forever now
> Be the moon's herald.

The poems of *A Wreath of Christmas Legends* are very much in the mainstream of McGinley poetry. These legends seem to be a continuation of the poet's search for meaningful concerns in literature, a search for ways to do more than belittle—rather, to build—for her readers. The typical understatement in each poem and in the series as a whole serves McGinley well: this art is based not on dogma or doctrine but on the always very human reaction to a more-than-human experience. The concern of each of these poems, shaped and figured with such evident care and warmth, is love.

II Sixpence *and* Saints

In 1961, under the title "The Sentimentalists," McGinley published a critique of modern writing. The authors whom she criticized were those who had lost proportion in their depiction of the world: "To overstress evil is as banal as to overemphasize goodness. . . . books put more burden on a single emotion than it is able to carry."[9] Referring to Tom Paine and Saint Augustine, McGinley complains that books *do* have influence and that this "flood of sickness" is bound to do damage, especially to the younger reader.[10] Perhaps because she is "sick to death of shock," McGinley has turned in her own prose to an entirely new subject—that of the Christian saints—and, again, to her earlier concerns of family and home.

Sixpence in Her Shoe, published in 1964, was McGinley's "reward" to the modern housewife. According to an English legend, a good housewife would sometimes find a sixpence in her shoe—her tribute for doing her work well. Divided into the sections about wife, house, and family, *Sixpence* elaborates on many of the same premises as *The Province of the Heart* (1959). There is more attention given to matters of housewifery per se—furniture refinishing, recipes, cooking tools—but the wholeness of the book removes any clinical tone from even the "wreath" of recipes.

For McGinley's theme in *Sixpence*, as in her earlier collection, is the "traditional concern" of woman—"Wifehood, the house, a family . . . each in its way represents one of the other great three—faith, hope, charity—which St. Paul sets down as the virtues of earth. (For how can one rear a family without faith? Or build a roof without hope? Or remain a proper wife without charity?) They are life's vital elements and no ordered world can endure without them."[11]

Frequently McGinley includes in these essays some mention of religious teaching or principle. Trying to decide how to convince a "progressive" grandmother that "manners are morals" brings her to the Ten Commandments. "The Pleasures of Thrift" stem from the true thrift, one motivated by ultimate charity—saving something so that it may be put to a better, less selfish use. And, as well as examples taken from her acquaintances or from history, McGinley uses saints: "Urbane gestures do not by themselves make philosophers or saints, but they do not unmake them either. In fact, the saints were almost all of them celebrated for courtesy. Francis de Sales, for instance. So silken were his manners that they almost obscured the hard fact of his holiness. Loyola charmed friends and enemies alike; Assisi's Francis was polite even to the wolves of the forest and the mice in his cell" (*Sixpence*, 228). Such allusions reinforce the spirit of the advice (and revelation) in McGinley's writing: they make the reader aware of the premises of the poet's own beliefs. They make more meaningful her emphasis on terms like *comfort, charity, love.*

In 1969, McGinley published a very interesting book, *Saint-Watching*. A "saint watcher, amateur standing," she writes in her customary casual but informative style of the real happenings, the real involvements of the revered Christian figures. In the earlier short poems, "Reformers, Saints, and Preachers," McGinley had focused on the humor, the telling single detail, which made each character memorable. In this book, humor has become compassion, the fullness of the lives treated bringing the weighty meaning of *saint* to the reader. It is as if McGinley has grown from thinking of these people as good subjects for poems to a view of them as real and admirable friends in themselves—a progression in attitude not unlike that between her early work with the Medieval Christmas legends and the later poems in *A Wreath of Christmas Legends.*

One of the most interesting chapters in the book is entitled "Good Companions," and in it McGinley describes the love that existed between saints and, quite often, a woman or a gentleman friend. Jerome and Paula, Clare and Saint Francis of Assisi, Vincent de Paul and Louise, Teresa and Saint John of the Cross—each pair's relationship makes the point of the poet's essay "that love of virtue does not restrict human love. The heart is an organ that can expand to hold the world. The more love it contains, the greater its capacity for containing extra supplies."[12] As she continues, "Ours is a carnal time, with every relationship suspect or explained away by psychiatry. It restores the spirit to learn that there can be friendships where nothing is asked and everything given; where innocence flourishes as if there had never been a Fall" (153).

Another of McGinley's concerns in writing about saints is capturing their wit, for history hints that these men and women were well supplied with saving humor. In a 1962 essay, "The Wit of Saints," the poet writes of the difficulties of making such good people interesting: "What a reader wants is not a picture, but a motion picture. The stir of life is missing, and so is the sound of a natural voice—the sigh of failure, the murmur of discontent, the ripple of human laughter. Most of all one misses the laughter."[13] That there is much wit, McGinley proves. That it is a truly humane wit, motivated by compassion rather than malice, comes through clearly in her descriptions. Her 1961 essay, "A Little Grace," makes clear that these men and women were human—they had to struggle against temptations, "doggedly blundering toward heaven."[14] That there are absurd moments, as well as magnificent ones, does not bother McGinley; for the acts of the saints, even if falsely reported on occasion, usually reveal their exceptional capacity for affection: "they loved much." McGinley tells many stories of the saints' friendships, among them that of Francis Xavier who cut the signatures off letters from his brother Jesuits and "pinned them inside his habit next to his heart."

"All saints do not suit all tastes,"[15] McGinley opens her 1968 essay "3 Against the Grain." Speaking of the strange Bernard of Clairvaux, Rose of Lima, and Simeon Stylites, she describes the times and conditions under which each lived. "The environment, the need, produced the person." McGinley recognizes, too, in her essay defending Saint Paul, that there are movements in the popularity of the various saints. A man's appeal depends on the culture which prevails at any given time. Ironically, McGinley feels, the man who created such an apt definition of love is "out of style" in today's professed search for that kind of charity.[16] It is interesting that in these later essays McGinley appears to be evaluating the saints from a wider perspective, in relation to their societies, with a wary eye toward her own environment. Yet, despite some sad references to the contemporary scene, she concludes "Good Men and Beasts" with the affirmation that saints must exist today, somewhere, living humbly, sharing what they have with human creatures and animals alike. "For while the old needs remain there will always be some good man to ease them. The patterns of compassion do not change."[17]

To identify McGinley as a saint watcher is not difficult. Aside from her expert retelling of the legends, her synthesis of the many fragments of story, such writing brings both reader and writer back to virtue. As McGinley explains, these are "men and women larger than life": "For Tennyson was right. The old sentimental line, 'We needs must love the highest when we see it,' is, like most sentimental savings, perfectly true. Virtue is man's Everest and those who climb highest are most worth admiring."[18]

III *More for Children*

As McGinley's own daughters, Julie and Patsy, mature, so do her books for "children." *Sugar and Spice, the ABC of being a girl* and *A Girl and Her Room* depict young ladies growing into femininity; and McGinley does so in rhymes marked by the now prevalent unexpected. *Aren't Boys Awful?* was published in 1961 with Ogden Nash's *Girls Are Silly*, and a comparison of the two poems makes evident the differences in the apt styles of each poet.

How Mrs. Santa Claus Saved Christmas, McGinley's dullest book for children—or so say some critics—appeared in 1963; her most controversial, *The B Book*, a year before. In this earlier story of "a small Brown Bee/ named Bumble/ who got tired of Being a Bee," it looked as though McGinley had gone back on her stand against the "limited vocabulary" books for children. Not so, the poet answered—and the book itself, though admittedly aimed at young readers, manages to maintain some level of interest. The story shows little Bumble being disgruntled ("a Bee is not Beautiful. . . . A Bee is only Busy"), despite arguments from Big Bee ("It is a Brave thing to Be a Bee"). Bumble is finally reconciled to his life through the argument that "Everything Best in the world Begins with a Bee (B)," through the word play on *Bee* and *B*—Birds, Bantams, and Baby chicks; Balloons and Boys on Bicycles.

In 1961 had appeared *Mince Pie and Mistletoe,* a recounting of traditional ethnic customs for celebrating Christmas; and in 1966, *Wonderful Time,* a collection of separate poems on time or subjects related to it:

> Time is peculiar
> And hardly exact.
> Though minutes are minutes,
> You'll find for a fact
> (As the older you get
> And the bigger you grow)
> That Time can
> Hurrylikethis
> Or plod,   plod,   slow.[19]

McGinley's 1968 anthology of poems for children, *Wonders and Surprises,* includes none of her own poems but draws from the world's best poetry—Walter de la Mare, Yeats, Coleridge, Shakespeare, Cummings, Theodore Roethke, Robert Frost, Randall Jarrell, Ogden Nash, Ezra Pound, Emily Dickinson, and many others. Her selection proves the truth of what she had indicated in a 1965 dialogue, that she felt like a scholar in her love for wide and various reading. Her Foreword to the book speaks with authority of the purpose of the anthology ("pleasure") and of poetry ("what cannot be said so well in prose") and then goes on to defend the inclusion of some incantations and curses, "poetry is chiefly emotion, and anger is as strong an emotion as love."[20] Her dedication, "For my children and theirs," suggests her comment a few years before that women view life differently than men do because of their ability to have children: "your children are your children even when they're fifty. You never really stop *having* them. . . . they're still your concern."[21] Even at sixty-three, Miss McGinley can identify with the child's imagination. She has made good choices.

IV *The Place of the Poet*

Through the forty years of her writing career, Miss McGinley
has borne her place as a "light versifier" (or whatever) with
great restraint. She has written few poems about poetry, or the
Muse, or herself as poet, or, greatest temptation of all, about other
poets. Those she has written—"Mrs. Sweeney Among the
Allegories," "Notes on Literary Revivals," "Literary Landscape
with Dove and Poet," and "Public Journal"—censure an insincerity
in modern writing. The poet who deliberately prostitutes the
poem ("it will be sport, writing my private hates/ And my
personal credo"); the poet whose pretensions drown his perspicacity ("though I understand Spain, I do not understand Span-
ish"); the poet of "fashion" in technique:

> I'll be casual with rhymes for that is the trend,
> Fashionable as the black hat of Anthony Eden.
> I may put them at the middle of the stanza instead of the end,
> For really amazing effect.
> Or perhaps I'll find that assonance heightens the meaning better.
> Yes, definitely, I prefer the latter.

> (175)

The poem which makes "many allusions/ To a daft system and
a world disorder" is also suspect, as is the one in which "music
needs no meaning."

Such objections are easily understood, when the reader knows
McGinley. Delight in the well-crafted poem, in the poem which
"says" what it intends (and whose intention is to reach its
reader), in the poem which reveals a many-sided picture, not
only the dark—this is the feeling of Phyllis McGinley, poet,
housewife, mother, saint watcher. McGinley's own "sanity," like
that of Alice, has stemmed from her lack of compromise and
from her conviction that she must write as well as she can,
technically, and as humanely as she can, emotionally. Whether
her poems be in satire or in praise, they reach toward a better
way for human nature. As for whether poems are light or
serious, McGinley wrote in 1968 that she draws "no line between
poetry which is written out of seriousness and that which has
been set down to amuse. Just as short stories or novels are still
novels or short stories whether they are sad or funny, so poetry
is still poetry no matter which emotion it arouses."[22]

It is perhaps fitting that one of McGinley's most recent poems
is a sonnet (a twenty-line sonnet, with the innovation now

characteristic of the poet), extolling the happiness of family com-
panionship. "The Day I Was So Happy" opens with a description of a common, sullen day: "It rained on and off all morning/
. . . . We drank black coffee." To the mother, however, the day
was "gilded round the edges/ Like halos of saints in Florentine
galleries." As the sestet shows, her duties assume the qualities
of ritual: "merely having the cloth for dinner that night/ Seemed
sacramental." Why? As we expect from McGinley by this time,
the simplest, most womanly, of answers: "And those I loved were
kind to me and each other."[23]

Writing so well about the simple matters of everyday living
is no easy task. In her ten volumes of poetry, seventeen children's
books, and two collections of essays,[24] McGinley has often risen
past the didactic stance that popular writing must, of necessity,
take. Most readers demand answers, the glib assurances and firm
absolutes of a past age. McGinley herself tends to depreciate her
accomplishment, in some ways, "In both prose and verse I am
chiefly a technician, a painstaking, hardworking laborer in
literary vineyards. My virtue is to beguile. While I preach, I
amuse. Perhaps, too, my verse, since it can be read by the general
public, opens doors onto wider vistas than mine—keeps in the
memory of non-poetry lovers the shape of stanzas on a page.
It may not be the Everest of attainments but I and my readers
will have to settle for it."[25] But, as W. H. Auden reminds us, if
McGinley's writings are "light" ones, "among the half dozen or
so things for which a man of honor should be prepared, if
necessary, to die, the right to play, the right to frivolity, is not
the least."[26]

After this close study of all McGinley's writing—forty years
of it—I should like to return to the business of differentiating
between light and serious poetry. There is much about Mc-
Ginley's poetry that is more "serious" than many poems being
written today. There is a respect for the traditions of the poetic
art form not unlike the reverence many a sane man holds for
his religion. There is an altruistic impulse too often belittled by
the younger artisans of modern poetry. And there are many
moments when McGinley writes excellent poetry, especially in
the 1950's. As Miss McGinley herself describes it: "Occasionally
I wrote better than I was able. The lovely achievement of rising

above my equipment happened to me when my daughters were adolescent—when I suffered and struggled along with them . . . a poem must mean more than it says."[27]

Because Phyllis McGinley's poems have meant more than they said for so many thousands of readers, she has been awarded nine honorary degrees, the Christopher Award, the Edna St. Vincent Millay Prize of the Poetry Society of America, and many other honors. A Pulitzer Prize-winner, Miss McGinley is also a member of the National Institute of Arts and Letters. She was one of two poets to read at the 1965 White House Arts Festival; and she has served on the board of *The American Scholar*. She has received these praises because she has written and spoken well—for the world of women as well as for the world of art, and, most important of all, for the world of virtue.

Notes and References

Chapter One

1. *Times Three,* Foreword by W. H. Auden. New York: The Viking Press, 1961, p. 87. All works cited are from this collection unless otherwise indicated.
2. Quoted in "The Lady in Larchmont," *Newsweek,* LVI (September 26, 1960), 120-21.
3. *The Province of the Heart* (New York, 1959), p. 105. Hereafter cited as *Province.*
4. "The Light Side of the Moon," *The American Scholar,* XXXIV, 4 (Autumn, 1965), 559.

Chapter Two

1. "The Light Touch," *The Commonweal,* LXXIII, No. 11 (December, 9, 1960), 277-78.
2. A. J. M. Smith, "Light Verse," *Encyclopedia of Poetry and Poetics,* ed. Alex Preminger (Princeton, New Jersey, 1965), p. 448.
3. *The Fireside Book of Humorous Poetry,* ed. William Cole (New York, 1959), p. 169.
4. "Introspective Reflection," *What Cheer,* ed. David McCord (New York, 1945), p. 316.
5. *A Treasury of Laughter,* ed. Louis Untermeyer (New York, 1946), p. 485.
6. *Ibid.,* p. 487.
7. *A Wreath of Christmas Legends* (New York, 1967), p. 61. Hereafter cited as *Wreath.*
8. *The Fireside Book,* p. 278.
9. *What Cheer,* p. 355.
10. *The Fireside Book,* p. 436.
11. *Ibid.,* p. 415.
12. *A Treasury of Laughter,* p. 4.
13. *What Cheer,* p. 318.
14. Clerihew is a form of comic poetry invented by Edmund Clerihew Bently. It consists of two couplets of unequal length and somewhat ridiculous rhymes to give a "potted" biography: "Sir Humphrey Davy/ Detested gravy./ He lived in the odium/ Of having discovered sodium." (*Encyclopedia of Poetry and Poetics,* p. 141).
15. *On the Contrary* (Garden City, New York, 1934), p. 36.
16. *The Fireside Book,* p. 451.

17. *The Continuity of American Poetry* (Princeton, New Jersey, 1961), p. 222.

18. *The Fireside Book*, p. 476.

19. *Ibid.*, pp. 492-93.

20. As quoted in "The Telltale Hearth," *Time*, LXXXV (June 18, 1965), 74.

21. " 'I Keep To Myself Such Measures . . .,' " *Poetry*, CIV, 3 (June, 1964), 137.

22. Conversation with Professor Bennett of Denison University, Granville, Ohio, 1965.

23. Address at Michigan State University, Conference on Twentieth Century Literature, 1965.

24. *O Taste and See* (Norfolk, Conn., 1964), p. 9.

25. "Christmas Eve under Hooker's Statue," *Contemporary American Poetry*, ed. Donald Hall (Baltimore, 1962), p. 31.

26. *Howl* (San Francisco, 1956), p. 23.

27. "Exercise No. 2," *Pictures from Brueghel* (Norfolk, Conn., 1962), p. 42.

28. As quoted in *Newsweek, September* 26, 1960, p. 120.

29. As quoted in Bernard Kalb's biographical note, *Saturday Review*, XXXVII (September 18, 1954), 11.

30. *Times Three*, p. ix.

31. "She Speaks a Language of Delight," *Saturday Review*, XLIII (December 18, 1960), 32.

32. *What Cheer*, p. 325.

33. *Ibid.*, p. 389.

34. *Newsweek*, September 26, 1960, p. 120.

35. "Andrew Marvell," *Selected Essays, 1917-1932* (New York: Harcourt, Brace, and Co., 1932), p. 252. As Eliot continues on page 261, wit is "an equipoîse, a balance and proportion of tones . . . it seldom exists, and is never recognized."

36. "The Cutting Edge," *Writer's Yearbook*, 1966, pp. 93-94.

Chapter Three

1. *Newsweek*, September 26, 1960, p. 120.

2. *Stones from a Glass House* (New York, 1946), pp. 88-89.

Chapter Four

1. "Suburbia: of thee I sing," *Harper's*, CIC (December, 1949), 78-82.

2. *Times Three*, p. xii.

3. *Ibid.*

4. "The Light Side of the Moon," *The American Scholar*, p. 558.

5. "Talking Down," *Wilson Library Bulletin*, XXXVI, 8 (April, 1962), p. 645.

6. *Ibid.*
7. *A Pocketful of Wry* (New York, 1940), p. 143.
8. *The Wide World of Phyllis McGinley* (pamphlet). (New York, n.d.), p. 3.
9. *The Horse Who Lived Upstairs* (New York, 1944), n.p.
10. *The Plain Princess* (New York, 1945), n.p.
11. *Wide World,* p. 3.
12. *All Around the Town* (New York, 1948), n.p.
13. "The Sentimentalists," *Ladies' Home Journal,* LXXVIII, 7 (July, 1961), 103.

Chapter Five

1. *The American Scholar,* 1965, pp. 556-57.
2. *Ibid.,* p. 558.
3. *Ibid.,* p. 564.
4. When Miss McGinley read this poem at the White House Arts Festival, June 14, 1965, she added this stanza for the occasion:

> Applaud both dream and commonsense,
> Born equal; then with all our power,
> Let us, forever, praise Presidents
> Providing Dream its festival hour.
> And while the pot of culture's bubblesome,
> Praise poets, even when they're troublesome.

5. *The American Scholar,* 1965, pp. 564-65.
6. *Poet's Choice,* ed. Paul Engle and Joseph Langland (New York, 1962), p. 73.
7. *The American Scholar,* 1965, p. 560.
8. *Ibid.,* p. 556.
9. *Poet's Choice,* p. 73.
10. "Frankly Sentimental," *The Writer,* LXIV (December, 1951), 399.
11. *Blunderbus* (New York, 1951), n.p.
12. *The Year Without a Santa Claus* (New York, 1957), n.p.
13. "I believe that children like recognizable pictures full of detail. . . . I don't think they like extremes in illustration where a house or a doll or an animal is distorted into some highly-decorative symbol. Modern art of this sort often robs a child of one of his chief pleasures in reading—the pleasure of recognition. Caricature for the child is a great mistake" (*Wide World,* p. 13).
14. *Lucy McLockett* (New York, 1959), n.p.
15. *The Most Wonderful Doll in the World* (New York, 1950), n.p.
16. *The Make-Believe Twins* (New York, 1953), n.p.
17. D. P. Hobby, "On the Side of Suburbia," *Saturday Review,* XLII (November 7, 1959), p. 41.

18. *The Province of the Heart* (New York, 1959), p. 179.
19. "Complaint," *On the Contrary* (Garden City, New York, 1934), p. 113.
20. "The Light Touch," *The Commonweal*, 1960, p. 278.
21. *Province*, p. 4.

Chapter Six

1. *The American Scholar*, 1965, p. 561.
2. *Ibid.*, p. 555.
3. *Ibid.*, note on p. 565.
4. "She Speaks a Language of Delight," *Saturday Review*, 1960, p. 32.
5. "The Lady in Larchmont," *Newsweek*, 1960, p. 120.
6. *Merry Christmas, Happy New Year* (New York, 1958), p. 34.
7. *Ibid.*, 36-37.
8. "A Christmas Legend," *McCall's*, LXXXVII (December, 1959), 28.
9. "The Sentimentalists," *Ladies' Home Journal*, 1961, p. 102.
10. *Ibid.*, p. 103.
11. *Sixpence in Her Shoe* (New York, 1964), p. 255.
12. "Good Companions," *Mademoiselle*, December, 1967, p. 122.
13. "The Wit of Saints," *Vogue*, CXXXIX (April 1, 1962), 124.
14. "A Little Grace," *Vogue*, CXXXVII (January 15, 1961), p. 60.
15. "3 Against the Grain," *Sign*, XLVIII (September, 1968), p. 42.
16. "In Defense of Saint Paul," *Critic*, XXVI (December, 1967-January, 1968), p. 17.
17. "Good Man and Beasts," *Critic*, XXIII (April-May, 1968), p. 17.
18. "A Little Grace," *Vogue*, January 15, 1961, p. 60.
19. "Lengths of Time," *Wonderful Time* (New York, 1966), n.p.
20. *Wonders and Surprises* (New York, 1968), p. 13, 14.
21. "Woman's Place Is . . .?" *Sign*, XLIV (July, 1965), p. 22.
22. *Wonders and Surprises*, p. 14.
23. "The Day I was So Happy," *McCall's*, LXXXVIII (September, 1961), p. 160.
24. The list should also include the lyrics for a 1948 Broadway revue, *Small Wonder*, and the continuity for the 1951 movie, *The Emperor's Nightingale*.
25. *The American Scholar*, 1965, p. 568.
26. *The Dyer's Hand* (New York, 1962), p. 89.
27. Letter from Miss McGinley to the author, mid-March, 1968.

Selected Bibliography

PRIMARY SOURCES

I. Poetry

"Ballade Against My Contemporaries" (poem), *The Atlantic,* CCX (August, 1962), p. 42.

"Ballade of Lost Objects" (poem and following statement) *Poet's Choice.* Eds. Paul Engle and Joseph Langland. New York: The Dial Press, 1962.

"A Christmas Legend" (poem), *McCall's,* LXXXVII (December, 1959), p. 28.

"The Day I Was So Happy" (poem), *McCall's,* LXXXVIII (September, 1961), p. 160.

Husbands Are Difficult. New York: Duell, Sloan and Pearce, 1941.

The Love Letters of Phyllis McGinley. New York: The Viking Press, 1954.

Merry Christmas, Happy New Year. New York: The Viking Press, 1958.

"The Night after Christmas" (poem), *McCall's,* VC (December, 1967), p. 42.

On the Contrary. Garden City, New York: Doubleday, Doran, and Co., 1934.

One More Manhattan. New York: Harcourt, Brace and Co., 1937.

A Pocketful of Wry. New York: Duell, Sloan, and Pearce, 1940.

"Banjo on My Knee" (poem), *Esquire,* LVI (August, 1961), p. 55.

A Short Walk from the Station. New York: The Viking Press, 1952.

Stones from a Glass House. New York: The Viking Press, 1946.

Times Three. New York: The Viking Press, 1960.

"Vanity of Human Wishes," *The New Yorker,* XXXVI (May 21, 1960), p. 38.

A Wreath of Christmas Legends. New York: The Macmillan Co., 1967.

II. Essays

"Beep, Beep," *America,* XCVIII (October 26, 1957), pp. 110-11.

"Busybodies Seem To Be Getting Busier," *Good Housekeeping,* CXXXIX (October, 1954), p. 49ff.

"Carrousels! Spring!" *New York Times Book Review* (March 29, 1953), pp. 24-25.

"Cook and the Book," *Saturday Review*, XLVII (October 24, 1964), pp. 61-63.

"Cooking To Me Is Poetry," *Ladies' Home Journal*, LXXVII (January, 1960), pp. 6-7ff.

"Flattery Can Get You Somewhere," *Saturday Evening Post*, CCXXXV (April 21, 1962), pp. 68-69.

"For Better, for Worse, but Not for Lunch," *Ladies' Home Journal*, LXXXII (February, 1965), p. 34ff.

"Frankly Sentimental," *The Writer*, LXIV (December, 1951), pp. 399-401.

"A Garland of Envies or 21 Reasons Why I Wish I Were a Man," *McCall's*, LXXXVIII (March, 1961), p. 57ff.

"Good Companions," *Mademoiselle* (December, 1967), pp. 122-23ff.

"Good Men and Beasts," *Critic*, XXIII (April-May, 1965), pp. 12-17.

"Inconstant Reader," *Good Housekeeping*, CXVIII (April, 1944), p. 22ff.

"In Defense of Saint Paul," *Critic*, XXVI (December, 1967-January, 1968), pp. 16-20.

"Lessons for Today: From McGuffey," *New York Times Book Review* (May 20, 1951), p. 9ff.

"The Light Side of the Moon," *The American Scholar*, XXXIV, 4 (Autumn, 1965), pp. 555-68.

"The Literary Larceny of Saint Columba," *Horizon*, X (Autumn, 1968), pp. 62-63.

"A Little Grace," *Vogue*, CXXXVII (January 15, 1961), pp. 60-61ff.

"Loafing: A Big Challenge to Men and a Laugh to Wives," *Life*, XLVII (December 28, 1959), p. 153ff.

"Mary Was an Orphan," *Saturday Review*, XL (June 8, 1957), p. 31. Related letter from Miss McGinley, July 13, 1957.

"My Affair with a Hatrack," *Good Housekeeping*, CXVIII (January, 1944), p. 23ff.

"New American Family," *Saturday Evening Post*, CCXLI (July 13, 1968), pp. 26-32.

"Part-Time Poet," *Good Housekeeping*, CXVII (December, 1943), p. 35ff.

"Party for the Little Ones," *Good Housekeeping*, CXIX (December, 1944), p. 39ff.

"Party Line," *Ladies' Home Journal*, LXXIX (December, 1962), p. 30ff.

The Province of the Heart. New York: The Viking Press, 1959.

"Reproachful Ghosts," *America,* CIV (March 25, 1961), p. 814.

Saint-Watching. New York: The Viking Press, 1969.

"*Saturday Review* Panel Takes Aim at *Second Sex*" (S. de Beauvoir), *Saturday Review,* XXXVI (February 21, 1953), pp. 29-30.

"The Sentimentalists," *Ladies' Home Journal,* LXXVIII, 7 (July, 1961), p. 23ff.

Sixpence in Her Shoe. New York: The Macmillan Co., 1964.

"Still Most Popular Word Game," *New York Times Book Review* (December 20, 1953), pp. 20-21.

"Talking Down," *Wilson Library Bulletin,* XXXVI, 8 (April, 1962), pp. 645-46ff. Reprinted from *Glamour,* 1960.

"3 Against the Grain," *Sign,* XLVIII (September, 1968), pp. 42-47.

"Whatever Happened to the Box of Candy?" *Good Housekeeping,* CXXX (May, 1950), p. 58ff

"What Every (Mother of the) Bride Should Know," *Ladies' Home Journal,* LXXXII (June, 1965), p. 57ff.

"What Is a Saint?" *Critic,* XXVI (June-July, 1968), pp. 28-35.

The Wide World of Phyllis McGinley (pamphlet). New York: J. B. Lippincott Co., n.d.

"Wit of Saints," *Vogue,* CXXXIX (April 1, 1962), pp. 124-25ff.

"Who's Who Cooks," *Good Housekeeping,* CXLIII (September, 1956), pp. 10-11.

"Woman's Place Is . . . ?" *Sign,* XLIV (July, 1965), pp. 22-26. With Sidney Callahan.

III. Books for Children

All Around the Town. New York: J. B. Lippincott Co., 1948.

Aren't Boys Awful? New York: Franklin Watts, Inc., 1961.

The B Book. New York: Crowell-Collier Co., 1962.

Blunderbus. New York: J. B. Lippincott Co., 1951.

A Girl and Her Room. New York: Franklin Watts, Inc., 1963.

The Horse Who Had His Picture in the Paper. New York: J. B. Lippincott Co., 1951.

The Horse Who Lived Upstairs. New York: J. B. Lippincott Co., 1944.

How Mrs. Santa Claus Saved Christmas. New York: J. B. Lippincott Co., 1963.

Lucy McLockett. New York: J. B. Lippincott Co., 1959.

The Make-Believe Twins. New York: J. B. Lippincott Co., 1953.

Mince Pie and Mistletoe. New York: J. B. Lippincott Co., 1961.

The Most Wonderful Doll in the World. New York: J. B. Lippincott Co., 1950.

A Name for Kitty. New York: Simon and Schuster Little Golden Books, 1948.

The Plain Princess. New York: J. B. Lippincott Co., 1945.
Sugar and Spice, the ABC of being a girl. New York: Franklin Watts, Inc., 1960.
Wonderful Time. New York: J. B. Lippincott Co., 1966.
Wonders and Surprises: A Collection of Poems. New York: J. B. Lippincott Co., 1968.
The Year Without a Santa Claus. New York: J. B. Lippincott Co., 1957.

SECONDARY SOURCES

AUDEN, W. H. *The Dyer's Hand.* New York: Random House, 1962.
————. Foreword. *Times Three.* New York: The Viking Press, 1960. A very masculine tribute to Miss McGinley as the most feminine of writers.
BROWN, R. M. "Open Letter to *The New Yorker*," *The Christian Century,* LXXX (July 31, 1963), pp. 956-57. Reply by D. E. Faust, September 18, 1963, pp. 1142-43; about the Xavier Rynne controversy.
CALLAHAN, SIDNEY. *"Sixpence in Her Shoe,"* *Critic,* XXIII (December, 1964-January, 1965), pp. 68-69. Praises McGinley's "humor, subtlety, and human wisdom" but objects to her curtailment of women's activities outside the home. See also "Woman's Place Is . . .?"
"Commuters' Special," *Time,* LVIII (December 31, 1951), p. 64. Favorable review of *A Short Walk from the Station.*
DOYLE, L. F. "Poems of Phyllis McGinley," *America,* XCII (December 18, 1954), pp. 320-22. Enjoys her poems for their evident "charity."
"Easiest to Love," *Time,* LXIV (July 19, 1954), p. 50. Admiring note on *The Love Letters of Phyllis McGinley.*
Encyclopedia of Poetry and Poetics. Ed. Alex Preminger. Princeton, New Jersey: Princeton University Press, 1965.
FREEMANTLE, ANNE. "Purrs of Normality," *Saturday Review,* XXXV (March 15, 1952), p. 37. Enjoys McGinley's tone of contentment in *A Short Walk from the Station.*
————. "Serious Frivolity," *The Commonweal,* LXI (October 22, 1954), pp. 69-70. Comments on McGinley's unashamed femininity, her "sympathy" with "the whole human condition."
GIBSON, WALKER. "Review of *Times Three,*" *New York Times Book Review* (October 2, 1960), p. 4. Discusses her view of life.
GRUNWALD, BEVERLY. "Review of *Sixpence in Her Shoe,*" *New York Times Book Review* (September 27, 1964), p. 20. Sees McGinley's view of housewifery as inaccurate; criticizes her assumptions.

HAYE, SARA HENDERSON. "The Cutting Edge." *Writer's Yearbook,* 1966. Good analysis of light verse, satire, and other modes of "cutting" expression.

HOBBY, DIANE P. "On the Side of Suburbia," *Saturday Review,* XLII (November 7, 1959), p. 41. Analyzes McGinley's prose style from the perspective of her poetry.

JACOBSEN, ETHEL. "Review of *Times Three,*" *Chicago Sun Tribune* (September 25, 1960), p. 5. Acknowledges McGinley's virtuosity, but is more impressed with her wit, variety, and "acute eye and ear."

KALB, BERNARD. Biographical note on McGinley, *Saturday Review,* XXXVII (September 18, 1954), p. 11.

"The Lady in Larchmont," *Newsweek,* LVI (September 26, 1960), pp. 120-22. Good profile of McGinley with several quotations from her.

McCORD, DAVID. "She Speaks a Language of Delight," *Saturday Review,* XLIII (December 10, 1960), p. 32. Perceptive discussion of McGinley's progress from the late 1920's to 1960.

MEYER, GERARD PREVIN. "Urbane Suburbanite," *Saturday Review,* XXXVII (September 18, 1954), pp. 11-12. Comments on light verse as genre and on its history.

"Moment with Phyllis McGinley," *Newsweek,* LVI (September 26, 1960), p. 120. Accurate interview with the poet.

O'BRIEN, MARY E. "Poet's Garden," *Popular Gardening,* XVI (September, 1965), pp. 20-23. Article tells of McGinley as wife, gardener, and homemaker.

PEARCE, ROY HARVEY. *The Continuity of American Poetry.* Princeton, New Jersey: Princeton University Press, 1961. Pearce's ambitious study includes nearly all American poets, as he attempts to find patterns in similarities and differences.

PINE, J. C. "Review of *Times Three,*" *Library Journal,* LXXXV (September 15, 1960), p. 3086. Admires the poet's technique but considers her style "garrulous."

"Poems to Remember; 'Soldier Asleep,' with biographical note," *Scholastic,* XLIV (March 27, 1944), p. 20.

"Real McGinley—interview," *Scholastic,* LI (September 29, 1947), p. 22. Biographical.

RICHART, BETTE. "The Light Touch," *The Commonweal,* LXXIII, 11 (December 9, 1960), pp. 277-79. Admires McGinley but also thinks her observations are superficial and, too often, flippant.

SANDERS, MARION K. "The Just-like-me Books," *Harper's,* CCXXIX (November, 1964), p. 149. Finds McGinley's prose "cloying," "imprecise," "arch," "snug."

SISTER M. GREGORY. "Review of *Sixpence in Her Shoe,*" *Best Seller,* XXIV (October 1, 1964), p. 251. Admires McGinley as Christian woman and writer.

SULLIVAN, K. "Phyllis McGinley," *Catholic World*, CLXXXV (September, 1957), pp. 420-25. Admires McGinley's prose style as well as her ideas.

"The Telltale Hearth," *Time*, LXXXV (June 18, 1965), pp. 74-78 and cover. Good interview with quotations from McGinley.

WILLIAMSON, S. T. "Review of *The Province of the Heart*," *New York Times Book Review* (October 11, 1959), p. 18. Admires McGinley's stand on most of the issues discussed.

WILLIS, K. T. "Review of *A Wreath of Christmas Legends*," *Library Journal*, XCII (September 1, 1967), p. 2931. Favorable, though Willis relegates the book to Christmas sales.

Index

128